AFTER SURVIVAL

After Survival

Shauntey J. Walker

For the girl who was creative, intelligent, and full of
possibility
but did not receive the attention, protection, or guidance
she needed.
For the girl whose gifts developed quietly,
whose questions went unanswered,
and whose becoming was delayed by survival.
This book is for you.
How you started is not how you end.
The woman holding this book is proof
that your life did not stop where love fell short.
Every choice she makes now,
every boundary she holds,
every truth she lives
is a devotion to you.
This is what it looks like
when the child who was overlooked
becomes the woman who leads.

Contents

Introduction

The Piano Bench

I was thirteen the day I learned what it meant to be alone in the moments I needed my mother most.

I had practiced for weeks for my piano recital—hours of progressions, scales, and songs I picked up faster than anyone expected. I was excited. My friends were coming. The choir director believed in me. And I hoped, more than anything, that my mother would feel proud.

But that morning moved slowly.

No sense of urgency.

No "We need to go."

No checking my dress, no smoothing my hair, no shared excitement.

Just the quiet, drifting silence I had learned to accept.

By the time we finally arrived, the recital had already begun. My name had been called. My seat at the piano sat empty.

And I broke.

I cried so loudly the whole church heard me—the kind of cry that comes from a place deeper than disappointment. Adults rushed to comfort me. The choir director apologized even though none of it was his fault. He later let me perform with the entire choir so I could still have my moment.

But my mother said nothing.

No apology.

No hug.

No softness.

Just silence.

That was the day I learned the truth I had felt for years, but had never been able to name:

If something matters to me, I have to carry it alone.

I didn't know it then, but that moment would shape how I loved, how I created, how I shrank, and how I learned to survive.

The Silent Mother Wound

The mother wound is not always loud.

It doesn't shout, slam doors, or leave visible marks. It doesn't always look like abuse. Often, it looks like provision without presence. Responsibility without tenderness. A mother who is physically there, but emotionally unavailable.

It is quiet.

It is subtle.

It lives in the spaces where nurturing should have been.

And because it is quiet, it often goes unnamed.

Many women grow up believing nothing "bad enough" happened to justify how deeply it affected them. So they minimize it. Rationalize it. Carry the confusion instead of the truth.

But emotional absence is not neutral. It shapes identity.

When the silence comes from your mother—the first relationship, the first mirror—it rearranges something inside you long before you have language for it. You learn to expect little. To need less. To downplay what matters before anyone else has the chance to dismiss it.

You can be gifted.

You just can't expect support.

This book is about that wound.

The Adaptation

Children adapt to what they are given.

Without consistent emotional safety, I learned to build my world inward. Imagination became a refuge. Creativity became a place where I could feel alive without interruption.

I didn't choose that consciously. It was instinct.

When the church started a music school, I begged to join. My mother signed the form, but her interest ended there. She never asked if I practiced. Never said, "Play something for me." Never told me she was proud.

But my fingers learned anyway.

I taught myself songs that were too advanced for my age. Other adults noticed. They encouraged me. They celebrated what they saw.

At home, the silence remained.

So creativity became my shelter. A place where I felt expressive, safe, and whole—without needing permission.

Many women develop similar adaptations. Some through art. Some through achievement. Some through over-responsibility, care-taking, or independence. These adaptations are not flaws. They are intelligence. They are survival.

But what helps you survive is not always what helps you live.

The Cost

I didn't understand the cost of being raised this way until much later.

It showed up quietly—feeling behind, unsure of myself, uncertain in rooms where other women seemed grounded in who they were. It showed up in relationships, in work, in how much space I allowed myself to take.

Eventually, one truth became unavoidable:

I wasn't flawed.

I was unmothered.

And that realization changed everything—not because it assigned blame, but because it restored clarity.

The Turn

Distance gave me perspective.

Not distance as punishment. Distance as truth.

As I grew older, I began to see the pattern clearly. I didn't want to repeat it. I didn't want to stay small to stay safe. I didn't want to bury my gifts under emotional silence or live my life negotiating for permission to exist fully.

I realized something essential:

Understanding the wound is not enough.

You have to stop reenacting it.

That realization didn't arrive as a dramatic breakthrough. It arrived as a quiet decision—to stop carrying what was never mine to hold.

That is where this book begins.

What This Book Is Here to Do

This is not a book about blaming your mother.

And it is not a book about endlessly revisiting the past.

This is a book about **ending the patterns that emotional absence creates**.

It is about learning how to stop shrinking, overgiving, performing, and surviving in relationships that feel familiar but leave you depleted.

It is about self-leadership—the ability to recognize what shaped you without letting it dictate who you become.

By the end of this book, you will not just understand what happened to you. You will understand why certain dynamics no longer fit—and how to choose differently.

The Arc of Becoming

This book moves through six stages:

- **The Silence** — where the wound formed
- **The Seeing** — where patterns become visible
- **The Settling** — where your nervous system finds safety
- **The Stirring** — where your voice and desires return
- **The Standing** — where your identity strengthens

- **The Becoming** — where you step into the life you lead, not survive

These are not steps to rush through. They are shifts in how you relate to yourself, your creativity, and your life.

You don't need to be finished healing to begin. You only need to be willing to see clearly.

A Welcome

If something in you tightened while reading this, pause.

You're not broken.

You're not late.

You're not behind.

You were interrupted.

And now, you are in the position to choose what comes next.

Your creativity was never the problem.

Your environment was.

But your becoming?

That part belongs to you.

Let's begin.

CHAPTER 1 - The Silent Mother Wound

What Emotional Absence Looks Like
When I think back on my childhood, the clearest memory isn't a dramatic event. It's a moment so ordinary that it took me years to understand why it hurt.

My mother would sit on the edge of her bed after work, arms crossed, eyes locked on the television. Her whole body held a tension that said she was present—but not available.

I would come into the room the way children naturally do—playful, silly, eager to connect. Full of whatever small joy I had gathered throughout the day.

And every time, the response was the same.

A sharp, irritated "Ugh."

A dismissive wave of her hand.

A silent request for me to disappear.

There was no yelling.

No confrontation.

No moment anyone else would call harmful.

Just the kind of irritation that teaches a child her presence is an interruption.

At the time, I didn't have language for emotional neglect or mis-attunement. I only knew that whenever I tried to bring joy into the room, it died at the door.

Little by little, I learned the rules of the house.

Be quieter.

Be easier.

Take up less space.

And without ever deciding to, I began shrinking to fit the emotional temperature of our home.

Children do that.

Growing Up Without Emotional Attunement

Some mothers are cold.

Some are explosive.

Some are distracted.

Mine was dismissive.

Not cruel in a way anyone would notice. Not the kind of mother people point to and say, *That's wrong.* She showed up physically. She handled responsibilities. She did what needed to be done.

But she did not connect.

She didn't ask questions.

Didn't look up when I entered a room.

Didn't mirror excitement or curiosity.

Didn't offer softness, guidance, or emotional presence.

She simply existed beside me.

For a long time, I explained this away. I told myself she was tired. Overworked. Not affectionate by nature. I normalized the distance because it was all I knew.

It wasn't until adulthood that I could finally name what I experienced:

Emotional neglect.

Not the dramatic kind that becomes a story people rally around. The quiet kind that becomes invisible—especially to the child living inside it.

What the Silent Mother Wound Is

The silent mother wound does not form through what was done, but through what was missing.

It develops when a child's inner world has nowhere safe to land.

This wound can exist in homes that appear stable from the outside. Homes with routines, structure, and provision. Homes without chaos, without screaming, without obvious harm.

But inside those homes, something essential is absent:

Emotional attunement.

Attunement is the experience of being seen, responded to, and mirrored. It is a parent noticing not just what a child does, but how she feels. It is curiosity about a child's inner life. Warmth without irritation. Presence without withdrawal.

When attunement is missing, a child learns quickly—without being told:

My feelings are inconvenient.

My joy is too much.

My needs have nowhere to go.

These lessons are not taught through lectures or punishment. They are absorbed through tone, through silence, through the subtle ways a parent turns away.

And children always adapt.

The Child's Adaptation to Silence

Some children respond to emotional absence by acting out. Others withdraw completely.

Sensitive, intuitive, emotionally perceptive children adapt differently.

They read rooms before they can read words. They sense emotional shifts before they understand language. They become experts in the climate around them because safety depends on it.

When a child like this grows up without emotional attunement, she learns to regulate herself early.

She becomes self-contained.

She lowers her volume.

She edits her joy.

She turns inward.

This inward turn can take many forms—imagination, competence, caretaking, creativity, achievement. The form varies, but the function is the same.

Survival.

This is not a flaw.

It is intelligence.

But survival has a cost.

Why Naming This Matters

Because the silent mother wound is quiet, many women never name it at all.

They tell themselves nothing "bad enough" happened. That they were provided for. That they should be grateful. That they're just sensitive. That this is simply how families are.

But emotional absence shapes a child whether it is named or not.

If you recognize yourself in these pages, it does not mean something is wrong with you.

It means you adapted to an environment that could not fully hold you.

Before we can talk about who you became, how you learned to carry yourself, or the patterns that followed you into adulthood, we have to pause here.

We have to tell the truth about the environment that shaped you.

Not to assign blame.

Not to rewrite the past.

But to understand what your nervous system learned in silence.

Before We Move Forward

This chapter exists to name the wound—not to resolve it.

If something in you recognizes this landscape, that recognition matters.

In the next chapter, we will explore the next question this truth naturally raises:

Who does a child become when she grows up unseen?

Because once you understand how identity forms without nurture, you can finally see why carrying yourself alone became second nature—and what it has cost you.

CHAPTER 2 - Growing Up Unseen

How Identity Forms Without Nurture
You don't always realize you grew up unseen until you encounter what being seen actually looks like.

Sometimes it's a small moment—a mother leaning toward her daughter with genuine interest, a parent asking a question and waiting for the answer. There's no performance in it. No rush. Just attention. And in witnessing it, something inside you registers the difference before you can explain it.

Not as memory.
As contrast.

Growing up unseen rarely looks dramatic. More often, it looks functional. The house runs. The bills are paid. The basics are handled. There is no obvious crisis to point to, nothing that signals neglect from the outside.

And because nothing appears broken, the child assumes nothing is missing.

It takes time—often decades—to understand that a parent can manage a child's physical life while leaving her inner life untouched.

Identity Without Reflection

Children do not discover who they are in isolation.

They learn themselves through response.

A caregiver's attention acts as a mirror, reflecting back not just that a child exists, but how she exists. Warmth communicates worth. Curiosity communicates interest. Guidance communicates safety.

When those reflections are inconsistent or absent, identity does not pause.

It reorganizes.

Instead of forming through recognition, the child begins forming through adjustment. She becomes oriented to what the environment requires rather than what she feels. She learns to monitor, anticipate, and adapt long before she learns to trust her own internal signals.

This is not a conscious process.

It is an intelligent response to emotional uncertainty.

Becoming Self-Sufficient Before Becoming Yourself

When emotional presence is unreliable, a child learns early that she cannot depend on it.

So she becomes the one she depends on.

She figures things out.

She regulates herself.

She learns how to function without guidance.

From the outside, this often reads as maturity. She appears capable, composed, responsible. She doesn't ask for much. She doesn't create problems.

But this is not selfhood.

This is survival competence.

Identity requires room to experiment, to be reflected mid-process, to try and fail without losing connection. Without that room, the child skips discovery and moves straight into performance.

Not because she wants to—but because there is no other option.

Sensitivity Turned Inward

Children who are sensitive, intuitive, and emotionally perceptive experience this absence more acutely.

They notice shifts in tone. They sense withdrawal. They feel when their presence changes the emotional temperature of a room. Over time, they learn what draws irritation and what invites distance.

So they turn inward.

The inner world becomes a place of coherence when the external one cannot offer it.

For some children, this inward turn becomes imagination.

For others, competence or caretaking.

For many, creativity.

The form varies.

The function remains the same.

Something internal steps in to do the work that attunement would have done—organizing feeling, meaning, and self-understanding from the inside out.

This adaptation protects the self.

But it also shapes it.

Early Capability, Late Identity

Emotional neglect does not prevent development.

It redirects it.

A child raised without consistent emotional presence often matures early in responsibility while remaining underdeveloped in self-trust. She learns how to manage life without learning how to rest inside herself. She becomes effective without becoming anchored.

This creates a quiet split.

She can handle things—but she doesn't know who she is while doing so.

And because capability is rewarded, this split often goes unnoticed. By others. And eventually, by the woman herself.

Competence hides absence well.

Why This Matters Before We Go Further

Before examining patterns, relationships, or behaviors, it's essential to understand the identity that formed underneath them.

You did not fail to develop a sense of self.

You developed one under conditions that required self-sufficiency instead of support.

In the next chapter, we will look at what happens when a child has to provide her own emotional structure—and how that early self-reliance becomes a defining force in adulthood.

Because once you understand **who you became to survive**, you can begin to see the cost of carrying yourself alone.

CHAPTER 3 - You've Been Raising Yourself

There comes a moment when something shifts.
Not loudly.
Not dramatically.
Not in a way anyone else notices.

It is quiet—almost unsettling in its clarity.

It's the moment you look back over your life and realize:

I've been the adult far longer than I ever got to be the child.

This realization doesn't arrive with anger. It arrives with coherence. With the sudden sense that your life, which once felt scattered or confusing, is finally arranging itself into a pattern you can see.

What you thought was strength.
What you thought was maturity.
What you thought was independence.

Was necessity.

The Illusion That Holds for Years

For a long time, the illusion holds.

You tell yourself you're just capable. Resourceful. Good under pressure. You take pride in how well you manage things. How little you need. How much you can carry.

But there is a difference between being taught how to stand and being left to stand alone.

15

The moment you realize you've been raising yourself is the moment that difference becomes impossible to ignore.

Emotional Starvation, Recognized Late

When you grow up without emotional nurture, you don't experience it as deprivation.

You experience it as normal.

You adapt to the portions you're given. You mistake emotional crumbs for meals. A nod feels like affection. A neutral response feels like connection. Physical presence feels like love.

And because you don't know anything else, your body adjusts.

You become efficient. Self-contained. Low-maintenance.

Only later—often much later—do you recognize what was missing.

Not through memory, but through awareness.

The Internal Parent

A child cannot survive without attachment.

So when emotional presence is inconsistent or unavailable, the psyche compensates.

Not consciously.

Not imaginatively.

But structurally.

An internal parent forms.

This internal figure does what the external one cannot: organizes emotion, provides reassurance, creates meaning, regulates distress. It becomes the quiet system that holds you together from the inside.

This is not fantasy.

It is adaptation.

And it works.

Until one day, you realize you've been doing far more than surviving.

You've been parenting yourself.

When the Pattern Becomes Visible

For most women, this realization doesn't come all at once.

It accumulates.

It shows up in moments that don't seem connected at first:

- realizing there's no one to call when you fall apart
- noticing how little guidance you received for adult life
- seeing yourself manage everyone else's emotions
- recognizing how familiar responsibility feels and how unfamiliar being cared for does

Eventually, the pattern reveals itself.

I've been holding what was never meant to be mine.

That recognition can feel disorienting. Even physical. Like suddenly standing still after years of motion.

The Collapse of Illusion

This moment is tender.

It often brings grief—not just for what happened, but for what never did. For the version of childhood you didn't know you were missing. For the care you learned not to expect.

And once the illusion collapses, something irreversible happens.

You can no longer confuse endurance with wholeness.

You can no longer mistake self-reliance for selfhood.

You begin to see your life clearly—not as a series of personal failures, but as the logical outcome of a childhood that required you to grow up early.

Why This Moment Matters

This chapter is not about healing.

It is about recognition.

Because you cannot change what you do not see.

The moment you realize you've been raising yourself is the moment you stop asking what's wrong with you—and start asking what you learned in order to survive.

In the next chapter, we will explore how this early self-parenting shapes your patterns in adulthood—how it influences relationships, creativity, boundaries, and the way you move through the world.

Because once you understand **what you became to survive**, you can begin to understand **what no longer serves you**.

And that is where the real work begins.

CHAPTER 4 - Why You Shrink

Overgiving, Loyalty, and the Loop of Takers
(The Shaping Stage)

You usually don't notice a pattern while you're in it.

What you notice first is that you're tired.

You notice that you keep doing more than you planned to.

That you keep stretching yourself thinner than you meant to.

That no matter how different the people or places are, the emotional outcome feels familiar.

At first, you explain it away.

You tell yourself it's just the season you're in.

That you'll rest later.

That this is just what commitment looks like.

But after a while, a quieter question starts forming:

Why does this keep happening to me?

This chapter is about that question.

Not as a personal flaw.

Not as a boundary issue.

But as a learned response that once kept you connected—and now keeps repeating itself.

When Usefulness Becomes Identity

If you trace the pattern back far enough, it usually doesn't start in adulthood.

It starts in childhood.

For many unmothered women, value was never something freely given. It was something implied—earned through being easy, helpful, or self-sufficient. Emotional presence was inconsistent, so usefulness became the safest way to stay connected.

Being needed felt like being allowed to stay.

So you learned to fill gaps before anyone asked.

You learned to anticipate needs before they were spoken.

You learned to become dependable, capable, and low-maintenance.

From the outside, this looks like generosity and strength.

From the inside, it's something much older:

If I am useful, I am less likely to be left.

How the Loop Reveals Itself

Patterns don't show up labeled as patterns.

They show up as repetition.

Different roles.

Different environments.

Different people.

Same emotional result.

You give more than is required.

Others take more than they should.

You wait for reciprocity that never arrives.

And when you finally try to step back—even carefully, even politely—the emotional temperature shifts. Warmth cools. Appreciation disappears. Tension enters the room.

That moment is often when the truth surfaces:

You were valued for what you provided, not for who you were.

This isn't about one relationship.

It's about a role your nervous system recognizes.

Why the Body Chooses What Hurts

At some point, you may wonder why you keep ending up in situations that drain you.

Why ease feels unfamiliar.

Why reciprocity feels rare.

Why you keep trying to "make it work" in places that quietly cost you.

This isn't because you're broken.

It's conditioning.

Psychologists call this repetition compulsion—the tendency to unconsciously recreate familiar emotional dynamics, even when they're painful. The nervous system seeks what it knows, not what is good.

If love once required guessing, performing, and enduring distance, then familiarity begins to feel like connection—even when it isn't.

Shrinking as Protection

Overgiving is usually easier to notice once you see it.

Shrinking is quieter.

It happens automatically. Without thought. Without debate.

You soften your voice.

You downplay your success.

You decide not to say the thing that matters.

You make yourself easier to consume.

Not because you lack confidence—but because you learned what expansion costs.

If brightness once led to withdrawal, shrinking became protection.

Loyalty That Costs Too Much

This is where many women get confused—because the behavior doesn't feel harmful.

It feels moral.

You stay longer than you should.

You endure imbalances.

You make excuses for dynamics that quietly drain you.

Leaving feels cruel.

Speaking up feels risky.

Choosing yourself feels like abandonment.

But this kind of loyalty wasn't taught as love.

It was learned as survival.

When attachment felt fragile, maintaining it at any cost became the rule.

The Creative Consequence

These patterns don't stop at relationships.

They follow you into your work.

You give ideas away too freely.

You build visions for people who don't honor you.

You stay behind the scenes instead of claiming the stage.

You prioritize others' projects over your own.

Not because your work lacks power—but because visibility still feels loaded. Space still feels like something you have to earn carefully.

This isn't humility.

It's reenactment.

The same choreography, playing out in a different room.

Where the Loop Begins to Loosen

Most people think patterns break through confrontation.

They don't.

They loosen through recognition.

When you see that overgiving isn't generosity, shrinking isn't modesty, and loyalty isn't love—the repetition weakens.

Not because you're suddenly different.

But because you're no longer unaware.

Awareness changes what the body is willing to tolerate.

Before We Go Further

This chapter isn't asking you to change anything yet.

It's asking you to see.

In the next chapter, we'll explore what happens when someone finally *does* see you—and why recognition can feel just as destabilizing as neglect when you've spent your life unseen.

Because once you understand the loop, the next question becomes unavoidable:

What happens when the silence finally breaks?

CHAPTER 5 - The Parent Who Saw Your Light

How Emotional Withdrawal Teaches a Daughter to Fear Visibility

Some wounds don't announce themselves.

They don't arrive through shouting or rejection or cruelty you can point to. They arrive quietly—through a subtle change in tone, a cooling of presence, a moment where connection thins for reasons you don't yet understand.

As a child, you don't have language for what's happening.

You don't know what envy is.

You don't know how emotional withdrawal registers in the body.

You don't know that some mothers struggle when their daughters begin to shine.

You only know that something shifts when you appear fully.

And because you are a child, you assume the shift is your fault.

The First Time Your Light Changed the Room

My earliest memory of this dynamic was small—so small I didn't understand its meaning until adulthood gave me the words.

My mother would hum around the house as she moved from room to room. Music was the first language I ever understood, so I was naturally drawn to it.

One afternoon, I joined her.

I didn't interrupt.

I didn't perform.

I didn't try to outshine her.

I simply sang beside her—a child reaching for closeness through sound.

And then something changed.

Her voice softened.

Her body withdrew.

The energy in the room cooled.

Not dramatically. Not in a way anyone else would notice. But enough for a sensitive child to feel it instantly.

Her presence faded.

In that moment, my nervous system recorded something it would remember for years:

When I shine, she disappears.

How a Child Interprets Withdrawal

A child does not interpret emotional withdrawal as envy.

A child interprets it as danger.

She assumes responsibility.

She searches for what she did wrong.

She adjusts herself to prevent it from happening again.

So I sang softer.

I took up less space.

I learned to modulate my joy.

And slowly, quietly, a belief formed:

My light costs me connection.

When Envy Doesn't Look Like Envy

Most people imagine envy as loud—criticisms, competition, resentment that spills into words.

Maternal envy is often none of those things.

It shows up as:

- flat responses to good news

- emotional distance after moments of pride
- silence following achievement
- warmth that disappears when attention shifts to you

It's polite.

Socially acceptable.

Easy to dismiss.

But creative children feel it immediately. We read tone the way others read language. We sense shifts before we can explain them.

You didn't know what to call it.

You just felt the room change.

She Felt Your Light Before You Did

Here is the part many daughters never hear:

Your mother did not need to understand your gift to feel it.

She sensed something emerging—an ease, a brightness, a natural expression that stirred places in her she never learned how to tend.

Not because she was cruel.

But because she was human.

Carrying her own silenced desires.

Her own unlived creativity.

Her own abandoned potential.

Your light didn't just shine.

It illuminated what she had buried.

And instead of moving toward it, she withdrew.

The Adult Moment That Confirmed the Pattern

Years later, the childhood confusion finally arranged itself into clarity.

I had saved money, booked studio time, produced my own EP, arranged the music, engineered the vocals, designed the artwork. It was one of the proudest creative moments of my young adulthood.

I handed my mother the finished CD with anticipation—not expecting perfection, just presence.

She accepted it without warmth.

She didn't ask questions.

She didn't listen.

She didn't say she was proud.

The silence was unmistakable.

That moment didn't create the wound.

It confirmed it.

This wasn't imagined.

This wasn't oversensitivity.

This was a pattern.

My brilliance didn't bring her closer.

It made her uncomfortable.

When Comparison Replaces Connection

Not long after, she bought herself a keyboard.

Not to connect with me.

Not to learn from me.

Not to share music together.

She kept it separate.

She didn't ask for guidance, even though I could have given it. She didn't invite collaboration. There was no acknowledgment of my skill.

The message was subtle, but clear:

Your gift does not bring us together.

How This Shapes a Daughter

Growing up in this emotional climate teaches a daughter something dangerous:

Visibility is unsafe.

Joy creates distance.

Brilliance threatens attachment.

So she learns to manage her light.

She dims it.

She delays it.

She hides it behind humility or service or support roles.

Not because she doubts her gift.

But because she learned what shining costs.

Seeing Without Villainizing

Naming this dynamic is not about turning your mother into a villain.

It's about telling the truth.

You can understand her limitations without denying the impact they had on you. You can hold compassion without erasing your experience.

Clarity does not require cruelty.

It requires honesty.

Before We Move On

This chapter is not about reclaiming your light yet.

It's about understanding why being seen hurts.

In the next chapter, we'll explore how to rebuild a relationship with visibility—how to protect your brilliance without shrinking, and how to stop tying your worth to whether others can celebrate you.

Because your light survived environments that couldn't hold it.

And learning how to let it exist freely is the work ahead.

CHAPTER 6 - The Breaking Point

The moment the chase ends — and self-abandonment becomes impossible.

I wasn't crying.

I wasn't angry.

I wasn't replaying an argument or grieving a fresh wound.

I was sitting at my keyboard on an ordinary night in 2020 — the same keyboard that had carried me through childhood loneliness, adulthood transitions, heartbreaks, breakthroughs, and the private inner world where my music had always lived.

Usually, my hands moved without thought.

I played to feel.

I played to breathe.

I played because music is the one place my spirit has never been interrupted.

But that night, I didn't touch a single key.

My hands stayed in my lap.

My body felt heavier than usual.

The silence in the room felt thick — almost shaped.

And in that stillness, without warning or drama, a sentence surfaced inside me with a clarity that felt older than my voice:

"I'm not chasing people anymore."

It didn't arrive with pain.

It didn't arrive with explanation.

It arrived like recognition.

Like something in me had finally stopped running.

I didn't realize it until that moment, but I had been holding my breath my entire life.

And that night, I exhaled.

THE BREAK YOU FEEL BEFORE YOU UNDERSTAND IT

People imagine breaking points as dramatic:

a fight,

a betrayal,

a door slammed hard enough to echo.

But creative women — especially unmothered daughters — often break in quieter places.

Our breaking point happens:

in stillness

in solitude

in the absence of chaos

in the moment our body finally feels safe enough to tell the truth

That night at the keyboard wasn't the break itself.

It was the **recognition** of a break that had already happened.

The fracture had been forming for years — across seasons of over-giving, emotional isolation, performing for love, and carrying hope that no longer belonged to me.

Breaking isn't always the moment you fall apart.

Sometimes breaking is the moment you finally stop holding everything up.

THE ABANDONMENT THAT WASN'T A SURPRISE

My mother cut me off in 2016.

No warning.

No softness.

No explanation.

I lost my housing, my grounding, and the last remaining illusion of what "mother" was supposed to mean.

But what shocked me most wasn't the abandonment.

It was the absence of shock.

Because somewhere deep inside, I had already been living as if her presence was temporary.

I had always been preparing for her absence.
Always holding the relationship together alone.
Always surviving on borrowed tenderness, hoping it would eventually become love.

Her leaving hurt — yes.

But the pattern beneath it was familiar.

The real breaking point wasn't when she left.

It was when I realized I no longer needed to go after her.

THE CHASE YOU DON'T NOTICE AT FIRST

Letting go of the person doesn't immediately dissolve the pattern.

I stopped chasing my mother —
but I kept chasing versions of her everywhere else.

In friendships that valued my usefulness.
In creative spaces where belonging had to be earned.
In mentors who loved my potential but couldn't hold my presence.
In romantic connections that felt intimate because distance felt familiar.
In spiritual environments where exhaustion was mistaken for devotion.

Even in my twenties, I reached for my father — again and again — hoping recognition might arrive from a different direction.

But ghosts don't turn around.

And chasing ghosts is just self-abandonment in a sentimental disguise.

That night at the keyboard, I finally saw it clearly.

I wasn't chasing people.

I was chasing:
closure
belonging
a childhood that never existed
the fantasy of being chosen without having to disappear
And I was tired.
Not dramatic tired.
Not emotional tired.
Bone-tired.
Spirit-tired.
Tired of rehearsing the same emotional choreography in every room
I entered.

THE GRIEF THAT DOESN'T START WHERE YOU THINK

People assume grief begins when the relationship ends.
But the deeper grief begins when the **fantasy** ends.
I didn't grieve losing her.
I grieved losing the idea of her:
the mother who would soften
the mother who would see me
the mother who would say, "I'm proud of you"
the mother who only existed in hope
Grief wasn't about absence.
It was about acceptance.
Accepting that she was never going to become the woman I kept
waiting for.
And once that fantasy dissolved, something in me finally had room
to stand.

THE FIRST REAL "NO"

People think the first "No" is spoken out loud.
It isn't.
The first real No is internal.
My first No wasn't to my mother.
It wasn't to a friend or a partner or a church or a role.

It was to the version of myself who kept chasing people who were never coming toward me.

I said No to:

the rescuer

the over-giver

the performer

the loyal daughter who survived on hope

the woman who believed love had to be earned

That No didn't argue.

It didn't explain itself.

It didn't apologize.

It settled.

Quietly.

Permanently.

Like a foundation finally poured beneath me.

BEFORE YOU TURN THE PAGE

This chapter is not about closure.

It's about cessation.

The moment you stop chasing what was never yours to repair.

The moment you stop reaching toward people who cannot turn toward you.

The moment self-abandonment becomes intolerable.

Before moving forward, pause and ask yourself:

What was the moment — even the smallest one — when your spirit whispered,

"I can't keep living like this"?

If you don't know yet, that's okay.

Sometimes the whisper begins here.

CLOSING REFLECTION — THE CHASE ENDS HERE

Breaking away is not betrayal.

Breaking away is the moment you stop leaving yourself behind.

You are not abandoning your mother.

You are not erasing your past.

You are ending the chase.

And when the chase ends, something essential becomes possible for the first time:

Stillness.

Truth.

Choice.

Chapter Seven begins there —

not with answers,

but with the slow, deliberate act of building a life that no longer requires you to disappear in order to belong.

CHAPTER 7 - Choosing Yourself

When I stopped chasing, the world didn't feel peaceful. It went quiet. For many creative women, this is the moment healing stops feeling active and starts feeling still.

Not peaceful.

Not serene.

Not soft.

Quiet in a way that feels like history.

Quiet that carries weight.

Quiet that feels older than the room you're sitting in.

It's the kind of quiet that makes you inhale deeper than usual because suddenly, there is nothing left to drown out the sound of your own spirit.

Most people call that loneliness.

But for an unmothered daughter, loneliness is never just a present-moment feeling.

Loneliness is a memory.

It is the echo of childhood — the stillness in the house after your mother's voice went flat, the heavy silence after your joy dimmed her mood, the thick quiet that wrapped itself around every moment you needed more than she could give.

So when adulthood hands you a season where the phone stops ringing, friendships drift, invitations fade, and you find yourself sitting alone with your own breath, your nervous system doesn't say:

"This is rest."

It says:

"This is danger."

Because to the child inside you, silence never arrived with safety.

Silence meant abandonment.

Silence meant you were on your own.

Silence meant love was not coming.

But adulthood quiet has a different purpose.

This chapter is where you learn to tell the difference.

A Clarifier Before We Go Any Further

Not every woman reading this chapter has gone no-contact with her mother.

Not every daughter has experienced physical abandonment.

Not every creative woman is in a season of literal isolation.

But *all* unmothered daughters — whether still in relationship with their mother or thousands of miles away — know the emotional landscape of being alone **in the presence of someone who cannot meet them.**

This chapter speaks to:

• women who feel alone *inside* their mother-daughter relationship

• women who experience emotional distance even during contact

• women whose mother is physically present but unavailable

• women who have stepped back, gone low-contact, or gone no-contact

• women who are simply entering a quiet season that triggers old emotional memory

You do not need to have left your mother to understand these dynamics.

You only need to have lived in the kind of silence that shaped you.

Everything from this point forward meets you where *you* are.

I. The Loneliness That Belongs to the Child

Loneliness is not the absence of people.

Loneliness is the absence of the person you needed.

It is the emotional residue of childhood — the way your body remembers sitting across from a mother who was physically present but emotionally unreachable.

When life slows down, when distractions fall away, when the room becomes still, your body reacts faster than thought:

No one cares.

Something is wrong.

I must be invisible.

I must have done something to cause this.

But you are not responding to this moment.

You are responding to all the moments that came before it.

This is why creatives often cling to noise — not because noise is enjoyable, but because noise is proof:

"I matter."

"I'm wanted."

"I'm needed."

"I'm not alone."

So you stay in friendships that drain you.

You overextend in relationships that no longer fit.

You tolerate company that adds nothing to your life.

You answer calls from people who only reach out when they need something.

Noise becomes a shield.

But it's a shield built for the child.

Not the woman.

The woman inside you needs something very different.

II. Isolation: The Intervention You Didn't Know You Needed

Isolation is not loneliness.

Isolation is rearrangement.

Interruption.

Intervention.

Where loneliness is a wound,

isolation is a clearing.

Isolation is what steps in when you won't walk away from relationships, environments, or patterns that keep shrinking you.

It is life saying:

"You cannot hear yourself in this noise."

"You cannot rise while carrying their expectations."

"You cannot grow where you have been performing."

Isolation often arrives abruptly:

A friendship ends.

A connection fades.

A group dissolves.

A chapter closes without your permission.

People you would have bent yourself to keep suddenly fall away.

At first, it feels like abandonment.

But in truth, it is alignment.

Isolation is the process of removing what your spirit can no longer hold — even when your mind still wants to negotiate its usefulness.

And once the noise settles, something surprising happens:

Your intuition becomes louder.

Your desires float to the surface.

Your truth stops whispering and starts speaking plainly.

Your creativity begins returning home.

Isolation is not punishment.

Isolation is preparation.

III. The Inner Shift That Turns Isolation Into Growth

Growth rarely enters loudly.

It arrives quietly, like morning light outlining the shape of everything you couldn't see in the dark.

It begins subtly:

Your shoulders lower.

Your breath deepens.

You notice you're no longer bracing for emotional impact.

Your nervous system begins resting in ways it never could around certain people.

Then deeper revelations appear:

That friendship wasn't mutual — it was maintenance.

That relationship wasn't love — it was habit.

That role wasn't purpose — it was performance.

That exhaustion wasn't random — it was information.

For creatives, this shift is life-changing.

Because most unmothered creatives live in two internal worlds:

The child who performs to be loved,

and

the artist who creates to be free.

Stillness is where the performer grows quiet

and the artist finally steps forward.

IV. Solitude: The First Form of Self-Belonging

Solitude is not loneliness.

Solitude is not isolation.

Solitude is chosen presence.

It is the moment you realize you enjoy your own company.

The moment you understand that peace is not a fragile thing.

The moment your voice, your breath, your intuition feel like enough.

Solitude is:

• emotional spaciousness

• a return to self

• a sanctuary instead of a sentence

• the birthplace of creativity

• the first environment where you truly belong

The child inside you feared being alone because alone meant you were unprotected.

But the woman you are becoming understands:

Alone means uninterrupted.

Alone means unperformed.

Alone means undiminished.

Alone means fully present with yourself.

Solitude becomes the place where:

Your self-trust rebuilds.

Your identity expands.

Your creative voice sharpens.

Your boundaries strengthen.

Your desires become honest again.

Solitude is the room where you meet yourself without distortion.

V. The Truth Beneath It All: You Were Never Afraid of Being Alone

You were afraid of what alone *used to mean.*

Alone used to mean invisible.

Now it means seen.

Alone used to mean unloved.

Now it means chosen — by you.

Alone used to mean empty.

Now it means spacious — a life wide enough to hold who you're becoming.

This is the shift:

Loneliness is the echo.

Isolation is the clearing.

Growth is the emergence.

Solitude is the arrival.

And when you reach solitude, something powerful happens:

You stop reaching outward for the validation you can now feel rising inside you.

CLOSING REFLECTION — THE DOORWAY BACK TO YOU

Take this in gently:

You were never abandoned in this season.

You were being returned *to yourself.*

Loneliness belongs to the child you once were.

Solitude belongs to the woman you are becoming.

Isolation saved you from the noise that kept you from hearing your own life.

Growth sharpened your vision.

Solitude opened your spirit.

And now you are standing at the threshold of a new truth:

You do not fear being alone anymore.

You fear abandoning yourself ever again.

In the next chapter, we step into reconstruction — how to break emotional loops, choose aligned relationships, and build a life that reflects the creative force you were always meant to embody.

Because now that you can hear yourself...

Everything is about to change.

CHAPTER 8 - Breaking Emotional Loops

Why We Return to What Hurts Us—and How to Finally Choose Something New

There is a particular exhaustion carried by creative women who grew up without emotional safety—a fatigue that does not come from overwork, ambition, or striving, but from repetition.

Not the repetition of tasks.

The repetition of emotion.

You find yourself living the same storyline in different bodies.

Having the same conversations in different rooms.

Reentering the same dynamics with new names attached.

This isn't coincidence.

It's pattern.

It's the loop.

But by now, you know something crucial: these loops aren't moral failures or emotional weaknesses. They aren't caused by softness or hope or a lack of boundaries.

Loops live in the body.

They are the nervous system's attempt to return to the first emotional environment it learned how to survive—whether that environment was safe or not. Familiarity feels regulating, even when it hurts. Especially when it hurts.

And for creatives, loops cut deeper. Creativity doesn't just express emotion—it amplifies it. You feel more, imagine more, interpret more, romanticize more. You turn wounds into meaning, longing into story, struggle into narrative.

When the wound is old, the story becomes circular.

This chapter is not about willpower.

It's not about cutting people off dramatically or proving strength through distance.

It's about the moment the woman you are becoming finally out-weighs the child you have been reenacting.

The Real Reason We Go Back

Most women think they return because they're unhealed or emo-tionally dependent. But what pulls you back isn't desire—it's recogni-tion.

Your body recognizes the rhythm.

The pace.

The tension.

If love once came with distance, then distance feels intimate.

If affection arrived inconsistently, inconsistency feels like possibility.

If connection required waiting, longing starts to feel like chemistry.

This is why you can leave someone logically and still ache for them physically. The ache isn't about who they are—it's about what they represent. A familiar emotional temperature. A known script.

Loops aren't maintained by pain.

They're maintained by pattern.

A Loop in Real Time

Imagine this moment.

You're working—creating, dreaming, focused. And then your phone lights up with a message from someone you finally walked away from.

"Hey stranger."

Your breath shortens.

Your stomach tightens.

Not because the message is meaningful—but because the rhythm inside it is familiar.

The loop doesn't reopen through big moments.

It reenters through small openings where a younger part of you still hopes this time will be different.

Why Creatives Stay Longer

Your imagination is your gift.

In trauma, it becomes the trap.

Creative women are especially vulnerable to emotional loops because you're trained to see potential where others see pattern. You feel intensity and mistake it for depth. You interpret emotional turbulence as meaning. You turn crumbs into storylines and hope into arcs of redemption.

But relationships aren't art projects.

And healing isn't a plot device.

Loops thrive when creativity becomes coping instead of calling.

When Belief Makes Pain Feel Sacred

For many women—especially those raised with religious, cultural, or moral conditioning—loops become fused with duty.

Forgive endlessly.

Family is everything.

Love means sacrifice.

Suffering makes you noble.

These beliefs don't just keep you stuck.

They make pain feel righteous.

Breaking a loop isn't rebellion.

It's reclamation.

You aren't betraying anyone.

You're refusing to betray yourself.

The Psychology of the Loop

Loops are reinforced by four mechanisms:

1. **Intermittent Reinforcement**
   Unpredictable affection creates addiction-like attachment.
2. **Fantasy Bonds**
   You love who they could be, not who they are.
3. **Trauma Repetition**
   The nervous system reenacts old wounds, hoping for a different ending.
4. **Inner Child Longing**
   A younger part of you still wants resolution through the same dynamic that created the wound.

Understanding the system weakens the spell.

But understanding alone doesn't end it.

When the Loop Tries One Last Time

Last month, my mother—the parent at the center of my deepest loop—appeared in my Instagram message requests.

No message. Just the notification.

My reaction wasn't emotional. It was physical. A full nervous-system contraction.

My first thought was clear and instinctive:

Leave me alone.

Not in anger.

Not in bitterness.

In recognition.

For the rest of the day, my body couldn't settle. Not because of her—but because of what her presence symbolized: a familiar doorway back into an old role. An old survival pattern.

And the truth surfaced quietly but firmly:

I can't return to something that would cost me the woman I am becoming.

I waited. I regulated. I checked myself. This wasn't fear. It was clarity.

Then I blocked her.

Not to punish.

Not to erase.

But to protect a life I've spent years rebuilding.

The loop didn't end because I blocked her.

It ended because I chose myself.

Awareness vs. Embodiment

Awareness says, *I see the pattern.*

Embodiment says, *I will no longer participate.*

Most people stop at awareness. Embodiment requires discomfort—the sensation of doing something unfamiliar but healthy.

Leaving a loop often feels wrong, even when it's right. Peace can feel suspicious to a system trained on chaos. Stability can feel flat. Safety can feel boring.

This isn't intuition.

It's withdrawal.

Your body is detoxing from emotional adrenaline. And your work is not to soothe that discomfort by returning to what harmed you—but to stay present long enough for your system to recalibrate.

This is where loops actually break.

When the Loop Finally Ends

The loop doesn't end when you leave.

It ends when you stop negotiating with fantasy.

When you decide:

I want the life meant for me more than the life familiar to me.

That's the rupture.

The moment identity outweighs history.

Questions That Break the Spell

Ask yourself:

- Does this relationship grow the woman I'm becoming or revive the child I had to be?
- Am I choosing this person—or a familiar wound?
- If this connection weren't family, would I still tolerate it?

- Does this feel like safety—or survival?
- What does this cost my creativity and clarity?
- Would I want my younger self living this way?

Few loops survive honest answers.

The Creative Cost of Returning

Creativity cannot thrive in vigilance.

Every return to a loop siphons energy, intuition, timing, and momentum. Not because you're weak—but because survival consumes resources creation requires.

Breaking the loop is emotional work.

It's creative work.

It's destiny work.

The Loop Ends With Identity

Not when you leave.

Not when you block.

Not when you declare yourself "done."

The loop ends the moment you decide who you are becoming.

My future matters more than familiarity.

I choose peace over adrenaline.

I choose clarity over fantasy.

That moment is sacred.

Closing Reflection — The Doorway Forward

Breaking emotional loops isn't punishment.

It's initiation.

You're not losing anyone.

You're releasing the version of yourself who needed what hurt her.

You're not rejecting love.

You're choosing a love that doesn't require suffering.

The loop ends here.

And in the next chapter, we rebuild the center of your life—your identity, your grounding, your emotional truth—so your creativity can rise from expansion instead of survival.

You are stepping into the woman your old loops were never meant to contain.

CHAPTER 9 - Building Worth Outside Of Family

Becoming Someone You Choose, Not Someone You Inherited

Breaking the loop doesn't immediately bring relief. It reveals something quieter and more enduring: an ache carried by women who grew up without emotional safety—an ache that follows them not only into loss or disappointment, but into moments that should feel like triumph.

It is the ache of accomplishing something meaningful and having no one in your lineage to hand the moment to. The ache of becoming someone your family never expected, understood, or nurtured. The ache of building a life from soil you had to cultivate yourself, while quietly wondering:

Who am I without the people who were supposed to name me?

Family is meant to be the first home of worth.

But for many creative daughters, family is where worth went un-named.

This chapter is not about rejecting family. It's about releasing the inherited belief that your worth must grow in the same place it was once denied.

It's about becoming someone you choose—

not someone you inherited.

THE COST OF STAYING IN ROOMS THAT SHRINK YOU

There comes a moment when a woman finally recognizes that openness does not equal safety.

Some rooms will never hold you, even if the door is unlocked.

You want connection.

You want belonging.

You want roots.

But each time you return to certain family spaces, you leave carrying less of yourself. Your body tightens. Your voice softens. Your boundaries blur. Your nervous system begins performing instead of resting.

Not because you are fragile—

but because the room is familiar in the wrong ways.

What feels like *"Maybe I should try again"* is often the body repeating an old sentence:

See me. Choose me. Protect me.

But longing is not direction.

Longing is memory.

Worth begins when you stop confusing the two.

A GROUNDING MOMENT: THE GRADUATION

I was thirty years old when I learned the truth this chapter is pointing toward.

I had spent years earning my master's degree—a full scholarship, a competitive fellowship, leadership roles, and a place at one of the top universities in the country. I met the Secretary of State. I led projects. I built something no one in my family had ever built.

One afternoon, I walked into my mother's room holding my graduation invitation.

I handed it to her.

She looked at it, then placed it on the nightstand without a word.

No congratulations.

No curiosity.

No warmth.

Not even the courtesy of pretending.

She didn't come.

I walked across that stage alone—surrounded by classmates whose families cheered loudly, and one friend who brought me flowers and told me she was proud.

And in that moment, something settled with finality:

If someone cannot celebrate you at your highest, they were never meant to define your worth at all.

Until then, some part of me still believed maturity or accomplishment might change something. But she didn't show up for the child. She didn't show up for the woman. She didn't show up for the milestone.

And that realization did not make me bitter.

It made me free.

DISTANCE IS NOT THE HEALING

In the months that followed, I learned something deeper:

Physical distance does not automatically create emotional freedom.

You can step away from family and still carry their silence inside you. You can leave a room and continue performing for it in your body.

Distance creates space.

But worth is built inside that space.

That's where the real work begins.

THE ROLES CREATIVE DAUGHTERS INHERIT

Many creative daughters grow up absorbing roles that were never chosen consciously, but assigned quietly:

The responsible one.

The peacekeeper.

The interpreter of emotion.

The gifted one whose excellence was expected but never celebrated.

Worth becomes synonymous with usefulness.

With contribution.

With emotional labor.

Your imagination—the same force that fuels your creativity—learned to compensate long before it learned to create freely. You fantasized that one day your mother might notice. That one day your effort might soften her.

But the graduation taught me the truth:

You cannot earn someone into becoming who they never learned to be.

THE TURNING POINT: STOP ASKING FAMILY TO NAME YOU

Every creative woman reaches a quiet threshold.

A moment when her spirit says:

I can't keep auditioning for belonging.

This moment isn't rebellion. It's rebirth.

Worth doesn't begin when you feel confident. It begins when you stop asking the wrong people to tell you who you are.

When you stop performing the daughter they expected and start becoming the woman you choose.

THE FOUR FORMS OF WORTH

Most women cycle through these forms before reaching the final one:

Inherited Worth

I am who they say I am.

Performance Worth

If I achieve enough, I matter.

Proximity Worth

If someone needs me, I have value.

Internal Worth (the goal)

I am worthy because I exist.

Internal worth is the foundation your childhood never built—which means your adulthood must.

WORTH IS SOMATIC, NOT THEORETICAL

You cannot think your way into worth.

Worth becomes real when it becomes felt.

It lives in your body as:

- shoulders that relax before you speak
- breath that deepens when you rest
- a voice that steadies instead of apologizes
- a spine that refuses to curl for anyone's comfort

Your body must learn a new sentence:
I am safe even when no one approves.
This is where worth begins to root.

WHAT CHOOSING YOURSELF ACTUALLY LOOKS LIKE

Choosing yourself is rarely dramatic.
It is cumulative.
It looks like skipping holidays when peace matters more than performance.
Texting a friend instead of your mother when you need comfort.
Resting instead of overworking to justify your existence.
Leaving conversations that shrink you—without explanation.

Each choice teaches your body:
I protect you. You can trust me.

THE CREATIVE CONSEQUENCE OF CLAIMING WORTH

When worth is outsourced to family, creativity becomes cautious.
It apologizes.
It over-explains.
It waits for permission.

But when worth returns home—to you—creativity shifts from performance to expression, from survival to truth.

This is when your creative identity finally stabilizes.

A FRAMEWORK FOR INTERNAL WORTH

1. **Inner Recognition**
   Becoming the witness you never had—letting your gaze land on yourself with tenderness.

2. **Emotional Protection**
   Guarding your peace with discernment, not walls.
3. **Identity Rituals**
   Practices that stabilize your inner world: music, writing, movement, solitude.
4. **Community Through Resonance**
   Choosing relationships based on alignment, not obligation.
5. **Creative Ownership**
   Letting your art express who you are—not who you were required to be.

THE WOMAN YOU ARE BECOMING

When a creative woman builds worth outside her family, something irreversible happens.

She stops shrinking.

She stops apologizing.

She stops inheriting identities that were never hers.

She becomes someone she can finally live inside.

And her creativity—the most honest language of her soul—rises without fear.

CLOSING REFLECTION

Your worth does not live in the house you grew up in.

Your worth is the house you are building inside yourself.

You are not defined by who did not show up.

You are defined by the courage it took to keep walking across every threshold of your life.

You are no longer continuing the story your family handed you.

You are authoring the one your spirit has been waiting for.

And now—

you can finally create from a place that is whole, rooted, and entirely yours.

CHAPTER 10 - Healing While Building

Why Your Transformation Happens in Motion, Not After

By the time you reach this point, you are already moving. You are building something — a life, a creative identity, a sense of self that no longer fits inside the old structures you came from. And somewhere along the way, you may have realized something unsettling:

Healing didn't wait for you to feel ready.

Healing rarely chooses a convenient moment.

It does not wait for your life to stabilize.

It does not ask whether your heart feels steady.

It does not check your calendar to see if you have space for another internal unraveling.

Healing arrives exactly where you stand —

mid-transition,

mid-responsibility,

mid-becoming.

For the creative woman raised without emotional safety, healing has never been optional. It is the body's insistence. It is the spirit's boundary. It is the moment something inside you whispers:

You cannot carry the old world into the new one.

This chapter is not about healing as a finish line.

It is about healing as a companion — one that walks beside you while you build your life, not after you've built it.

You do not heal first and build later.

You heal **because** you build.

You heal **while** you build.

You heal in motion.

THE SHIFT INTO INNER SAFETY: A NEW STAGE OF HEALING

Until now, your healing has largely lived in awareness — naming patterns, understanding your history, recognizing the shape of your wound, reclaiming your worth.

That work mattered. It still matters.

But something begins to change here.

This stage of healing is not primarily emotional or intellectual. It is **physiological**. Your nervous system becomes the classroom. Safety stops being an idea and starts becoming something your body can feel — sometimes slowly, sometimes unevenly, sometimes through contrast.

Creative women often try to *think* their way into healing. But your healing is not waiting in more insight.

Your healing is waiting in your body.

Your body is where the mother wound settled.

Your body is where emotional vigilance learned its rhythms.

Your body is where safety was first lost — and where it must now be rebuilt.

This is the point where healing drops out of theory and into lived experience.

THE SPLIT BETWEEN YOUR GROWTH AND YOUR BODY

Every creative daughter eventually encounters this contradiction:

Your mind has matured.

Your vision has expanded.

Your talent is undeniable.

Your spirit is awakening.

But your body still reacts as if the original danger remains.

You feel it in subtle ways — tension before speaking your truth, a stomach drop when someone pulls away, the instinct to overexplain, exhaustion that appears without warning, the reflex to shrink in rooms where you should be standing fully.

Your body is not betraying you.

Your body is remembering.

It remembers silence being followed by withdrawal.

It remembers joy being met with cooling.

It remembers shrinking as protection.

It remembers love arriving with conditions attached.

Your mind may know your childhood is over.

Your body is still learning that safety no longer has to be earned.

Healing begins when you stop demanding your body "move on" and instead offer it a quieter, steadier message:

You're safe now. I'm here. We're not going back.

THE SOMATIC TRUTH: HEALING BEGINS WHERE WORDS END

Somatic repair is not mystical. It is not performative. It is not something you "do right."

It is the gradual retraining of your nervous system to believe a new truth:

the danger has passed.

This truth enters the body in small, unremarkable ways — breath dropping lower, shoulders releasing before you notice, rest arriving without guilt, moments of quiet that don't immediately trigger panic. These shifts may feel ordinary, but they are not insignificant.

They are the body receiving its first adult message:

We are not living in that house anymore.

As your system softens, your creativity widens.

As your breath deepens, your intuition returns.

As your nervous system feels safer, your artistic identity rises.

This is why healing cannot be postponed until after you build your life.

Your expansion depends on it.

THE EMOTIONAL REALITY OF HEALING WHILE BECOMING

Here is the part most people don't tell you:

Healing while building is not graceful.

It can look like crying in the morning and showing up to your dream in the afternoon. Feeling an emotional flashback triggered by something small. Mourning your childhood while editing your work. Signing contracts with shaking hands. Feeling joy and fear arrive in the same breath.

This is not instability.

This is **integration**.

An old identity is loosening.

A new self is forming.

Survival strategies are losing power.

Your nervous system is relearning safety.

"Too much" is not a sign you are failing.

"Too much" is often a sign you are becoming.

WHEN THE OLD SELF BEGINS TO RELEASE

As your system stabilizes, emotions that were once unsafe begin to surface — not to overwhelm you, but because your body finally believes it can survive them.

Tears come not as collapse, but as unclogging.

Anger surfaces not to destroy, but to protect.

Sadness deepens not to drown you, but to recover what was buried.

Clarity sharpens not as punishment, but as guidance.

This is not unraveling.

This is release.

DISCIPLINE AS SELF-MOTHERING

For the unmothered creative woman, discipline takes on a different meaning.

It is no longer about force or control.

It becomes consistency.

Containment.

Care.

Small, steady actions — nourishment, rest, movement, tending your space, keeping your word to yourself — become proof to your nervous system that something new is happening now.

These are not aesthetic habits.

They are stabilizers.

They quietly communicate:

I will take care of us.

I won't abandon you.

You can rely on me now.

For a daughter who never experienced steady nurture, discipline becomes the first experience of steady love.

HEALING DOES NOT PRECEDE YOUR LIFE — IT WALKS WITH IT

There is something sacred in this stage of becoming.

Healing does not begin once you move.

Healing begins **because** you move.

Clarity arrives after the step.

Courage forms once you walk.

Alignment meets you after you choose.

Your calling does not wait for you to be healed.

Your calling draws healing out of you.

CREATIVE WOMEN HEAL THROUGH EXPRESSION

You do not need to be whole to create.

You need to be honest.

Creative women heal through voice, movement, story, song, breath. You create while grieving. You build while trembling. You rise while still learning how to feel safe.

This is not weakness.

This is embodiment.

This is integration.

This is rebirth in motion.

CLOSING REFLECTION — WALKING WITH HEALING

Healing while building is not a burden.

It is an initiation.

Into deeper self-trust.

Into embodied creativity.

Into a nervous system that no longer lives in the past.

Into an identity your childhood could not give you.

You are not behind.

You are not broken.

You are being rebuilt — step by step — in the middle of real life.

Not after the fear dissolves.

Not once the tears stop.

Not when you finally feel ready.

But here.

Now.

In motion.

And in the next chapter, we step into one of the most intimate stages of this journey — reparenting yourself, not as something to fix, but as a life you are finally ready to love.

CHAPTER 11 - The Art of Reparenting Yourself

Relearning Safety, Reclaiming Structure, Rebuilding the Self You Never Had Permission to Become

By the time you arrive here, something important has already changed.

Your body is beginning to recognize safety.

Your spirit is no longer negotiating for survival.

And the question is no longer *what happened to me*—

but *how do I live inside myself now?*

This is where reparenting begins.

Not as a concept.

Not as a strategy.

But as a lived relationship with yourself.

Reparenting does not start with a plan.

It starts with a reckoning.

A reckoning with the truth that the ache you carried was not only about what your mother couldn't give you—

it was also about what no one ever showed you how to give yourself.

There comes a moment in every woman's healing when longing shifts.

The hope that someone else will finally arrive softens into a quieter, steadier realization:

No one is coming.

And still—I am here.

Not as punishment.

Not because you are alone.

But because you have finally become someone capable of staying.

Reparenting is the moment you stop waiting for life to feel safe and begin creating safety from the inside out.

THE FRUSTRATION NO ONE TALKS ABOUT

Before reparenting feels empowering, it often feels unfair.

There is a grief-laced frustration many unmothered daughters carry—rarely spoken, deeply felt.

The frustration of realizing how much time it takes to rebuild what was never modeled.

The exhaustion of learning emotional basics that others inherited quietly, without effort.

You may notice the thought rise:

While other people were building lives, I was busy repairing my foundation.

You may feel behind.

Late.

As though adulthood arrived before you were properly equipped to live it.

But here is the truth few women name clearly:

Reparenting is not evidence of delay.

It is evidence of resilience.

Many people never survive the weight of early emotional neglect.

Some disappear into addiction.

Some collapse into numbness.

Some build entire lives without ever feeling safe inside them.

The fact that you are here—doing this work—means you refused to collapse where someone else did.

You are not behind.

You are ending a cycle your mother could not.

Even if she lacked language for healing, she knew pain.

Pain always teaches.

Some people look away from the lesson.

You did not.

Reparenting begins the moment you decide that what wounded you will end with you.

GRIEF IS NOT REGRESSION—IT IS ENTRY

Before reconstruction comes grief.

Grief for the guidance you never received.

Grief for the years spent improvising adulthood.

Grief for the version of yourself who had to grow up without protection.

This grief is not a step backward.

It is the doorway forward.

Grief signals that you are no longer minimizing what happened.

You are no longer calling neglect "normal."

You are no longer carrying the wound alone.

And once grief opens, something else opens with it:

Space.

Space for a new self to emerge—

a self your childhood could not create,

but your adulthood now can.

YOU WERE NOT CONFUSED—YOU WERE UNMODELED

There is a quiet devastation that arrives in adulthood when you realize how under-taught you were.

Not because you lacked ability—

but because no one demonstrated emotional adulthood for you.

You see it in moments like:

- apologizing for taking up space
- staying too long where you are diminished
- confusing chaos for connection
- hesitating when setting boundaries

- shrinking around confident women
- feeling unsafe asking for what you deserve

These are not character flaws.

They are evidence of being unmodeled.

Reparenting begins when you stop blaming yourself
for the education you were never given.

REPARENTING IS NOT A CHECKLIST—IT IS A RELATIONSHIP

High-achieving women often want steps, systems, and certainty.
But your nervous system does not heal through efficiency.

Reparenting is relational.

Your younger selves surface in waves:

- the child who was never protected
- the child who learned to perform
- the child who disappeared to stay safe
- the child who believed love must be earned

They do not arrive on schedule.

They appear when your body finally feels safe enough to let them be seen.

Reparenting asks only one thing of you:

Stay.

Stay present.

Stay compassionate.

Stay in relationship with the parts of you that were once left alone.

YOUR INNER CHILD IS ALSO YOUR GENIUS

For creative women, reparenting carries a deeper truth:

The child who was wounded
is the same child who creates.

She imagined worlds when the real one felt unsafe.

She turned silence into story.

She transformed survival into art.

The trembling child and the brilliant artist are the same source.

When you reparent yourself, you do not just heal her.

You liberate her.

You give her safety to take risks.

Structure to develop mastery.

Belief to keep going when no one claps.

Reparenting does not only close the wound.

It strengthens the gift.

THIS IS NOT ABOUT FIXING THE PAST—IT IS ABOUT CONSTRUCTING YOUR ADULTHOOD

You cannot retroactively give yourself a different childhood.

You do not need to.

Reparenting is not about reliving the past.

It is about building a future that was once impossible.

You are not catching up.

You are beginning.

And like all creative acts, this one starts without a map.

THE THREE FOUNDATIONS OF REPARENTING

Reparenting rests on three internal pillars—simple, steady, and lived.

1. Safety — *Am I safe?*

Every boundary you honor, every red flag you trust, every moment you protect your peace, your body hears:

You're safe with me now.

2. Structure — *What comes next?*

Structure quiets chaos.

Routines, rituals, financial clarity, emotional check-ins—these are not rigidity.

They are reassurance.

3. Belief — *Who am I becoming?*

Belief is the voice your younger self never heard.

It celebrates effort.

It affirms identity.

It reinforces becoming.

This is not perfection.

This is consistency.

YOU WERE NEVER LATE—YOU WERE DEVELOPING

What looked like detours were curriculum.

What felt like delay was preparation.

You built yourself in real time.

You learned while walking.

Reparenting does not suddenly transform you.

It changes how you stay.

Slowly, then unmistakably:

- you stop apologizing for existing
- you stop chasing chaos
- you say no without collapse
- you treat yourself with dignity

Your life becomes calmer because you became calm to yourself.

CLOSING REFLECTION — BECOMING THE MOTHER OF YOUR OWN BECOMING

Reparenting is not about replacing your mother.

It is about reclaiming yourself.

You are not doing this because you were broken.

You are doing this because you were unfinished.

Now, with hard-earned wisdom,

you are building the foundation your childhood could not give you.

You are becoming someone you can trust.

You are becoming the home you never had.

You are becoming the mother of your own becoming.

And because of that,
you now have the safety, clarity, and strength
to examine the relationship patterns shaped by the mother wound—
not with fear,
but with authority.

That is where we go next.

CHAPTER 12 - The Discipline Era

Embodiment, Capacity, Nervous System Safety, and Becoming a Woman Your Body Can Trust

By the time you arrive here, you already know something important:

you cannot think your way into safety.

There comes a moment in every creative woman's healing when the body begins to speak louder than the mind—not through panic or collapse, but through a quiet, insistent knowing:

I want to feel like home again.

For years, most of us tried to heal from the neck up.

We named our wounds.

Mapped our patterns.

Read the books.

Did the work.

None of it was wrong.

But none of it could finish the job.

Because healing is not conceptual.

Healing is not philosophical.

Healing is not something your body agrees to just because your mind understands it.

Before you ever had language for the mother wound, your body was already carrying it.

In posture.

In breath.

In tension.

In collapse.

In vigilance.

Your body lived the story long before you could tell it.

The Discipline Era is the season where you stop leaving your body behind

and begin building a life it can actually live inside.

Not through force.

Not through aesthetics.

Not through punishment.

But through trust.

WHEN EXPANSION OUTPACES CAPACITY

Every creative woman reaches a point where her inner expansion outgrows what her body can hold.

This is often misread as laziness, resistance, or failure—but it isn't.

It's a capacity gap.

I remember waking up one morning and realizing that my vision had outgrown my nervous system.

Emotionally, I had shifted.

Spiritually, I was expanding.

But physically, my body was still bracing for a world that no longer existed.

Nothing dramatic happened.

No breakdown.

No revelation.

Just a quiet clarity:

If I want a life different from my childhood, my body has to become someone I trust.

That was the beginning of my Discipline Era.

Not as control.

As partnership.

A promise I hadn't known how to make before:

I will not abandon you again.

HOW TRAUMA TEACHES US TO LEAVE THE BODY

When you grow up without emotional safety, the body becomes the first thing you leave.

Not intentionally.

Instinctively.

You feed it when you remember.

Rest it when you crash.

Override hunger.

Ignore fatigue.

Dress to disappear.

Move to survive, not to feel.

If your mother ignored her own limits, needs, and joy, you inherit not her biology—but her orientation toward the body.

This is not laziness.

It is lineage.

The Discipline Era begins when you realize:

your body is not the obstacle to healing.

your body is the place healing must land.

WHAT DISCIPLINE ACTUALLY IS (AND IS NOT)

Discipline has been misbranded for most women—especially creative ones.

So let's be precise.

The Discipline Era is not:

- fitness culture
- weight loss
- optimization
- self-surveillance
- aesthetic control

• punishment dressed as productivity

It is about **capacity**, not appearance.

A dysregulated body cannot hold a regulated life.

A depleted body cannot sustain creativity, visibility, leadership, or love.

You are not preparing your body for the world's gaze.

You are preparing it for your own expansion.

Discipline, at its core, is consistency with compassion.

It is the daily evidence your body needs in order to believe:

I am safe with you.

A FRAMEWORK THAT ADAPTS TO REAL BODIES

The Discipline Era is not a program.

It is a philosophy—one that adapts across ability, illness, energy levels, and seasons.

Here is the structure that holds it together:

Reconnection

Noticing your body again.

Returning attention before demanding change.

Regulation

Creating internal safety through rhythm, gentleness, and repetition—not intensity.

Strength

Expanding capacity slowly, in ways your body consents to.

Strength is not force. It is trust built over time.

Nourishment

Feeding yourself as an act of mothering, not control.

Eating enough. Choosing ease when needed. Accepting help when appropriate.

Presentation

Re-entering your own life visually, at your pace.

Not for others—but to signal presence to yourself.

Capacity

Preparing your body to hold the life you are becoming—creatively, relationally, spiritually.

This framework is not hierarchical.

You don't "graduate" through it.

You cycle through it—as needed, as able, as alive.

WHY THIS ERA CHANGES EVERYTHING

When your body begins to trust you again, healing accelerates.

Not because you're trying harder—

but because your nervous system finally believes it doesn't have to stay on guard.

That's when memories surface.

Emotion releases.

Intuition sharpens.

Creativity stabilizes.

You are not regressing.

You are integrating.

This is why the Discipline Era is not restrictive.

It is liberating.

Your body becomes the place your life can land.

CLOSING REFLECTION — DISCIPLINE AS DEVOTION

This is not a story about transforming your body into something else.

It is about transforming your relationship with the body that carried you through everything.

The Discipline Era is slow.

Intimate.

Sacred.

It is how you become the mother your body never had.

And when your nervous system begins to trust you—

when the bracing dissolves,

when breath deepens,

when presence stabilizes—

you stop performing worthiness
and begin **embodying** it.

This is not about becoming disciplined.

It is about becoming dependable—to yourself.

And your body has been waiting for that woman all along.

CHAPTER 13 - Nervous System Safety

How the Body Learns to Stop Bracing, Start Trusting, and Finally Breathe Again

By now, you've likely noticed something important:

your understanding has grown faster than your body's sense of ease.

You can name the patterns.

You can see the history.

You can recognize what shaped you.

And still — your body reacts as if it's living in an earlier time.

This is the moment many creative women reach quietly, without drama or language for it:

My body is still living in yesterday, even though my life is happening today.

For women raised in emotional unpredictability, hypervigilance becomes second nature.

It begins before adulthood. Before ambition. Before creativity ever becomes a calling.

It begins in childhood —

where attention became protection,

where bracing became instinct,

where reading the room became survival.

Hypervigilance is not a personality flaw.

It is a nervous system adaptation.

It is the body saying, *"I will keep you safe — even if it exhausts me."*

This chapter is where that effort is honored —

and where the body is gently taught that survival is no longer the job.

Safety is.

WHY HYPERVIGILANCE BECAME YOUR NORMAL

Growing up without emotional consistency teaches the nervous system to stay ahead of danger.

Before you had language, your body learned to:

scan tone,

anticipate shifts,

track emotional weather,

prepare for withdrawal before it arrived.

That vigilance later looked like emotional intelligence.

It became intuition.

It became perception.

It even became creativity.

But beneath the brilliance was a quiet cost:

The little girl who learned to read the room never learned how to rest inside it.

She grew up gifted, perceptive, and capable —

but safety never became internal.

What we often call "intuition" in these moments is something else entirely.

It is fear dressed as foresight.

Your body wasn't wise because it wanted to be.

It was vigilant because it had to be.

HYPERVIGILANCE IS NOT WHO YOU ARE — IT IS WHAT YOUR BODY LEARNED

Trauma-informed research describes the nervous system as predictive by nature.

It reacts before thought, prepares before evaluation.

This is biology — not pathology.

Your body is not overreacting.
It is overprotecting.
It remembers:
the raised voice,
the emotional withdrawal,
the silence that followed joy,
the rules that shifted without explanation.

Hypervigilance feels like intuition because it *once kept you safe*.
But what protected you then cannot lead you now.

Softening is not losing discernment.
It is learning safety.

And that learning begins here.

THE CREATIVE COST OF A BRACED NERVOUS SYSTEM

Hypervigilance narrows the body.
It restricts flow.
It limits risk.
It makes visibility feel dangerous.
It turns rest into guilt and expansion into threat.

A hypervigilant creative woman does not lack talent.
She lacks internal permission.

Permission to soften.
Permission to trust.
Permission to create without preparing for impact.

Creativity requires openness.
Hypervigilance requires contraction.

This chapter is where those two stop being enemies.

WHAT SAFETY ACTUALLY FEELS LIKE — AND WHY IT CAN FEEL UNSETTLING

Many women mistake relief or numbness for safety.
Safety is different.

Safety feels like:
a breath that drops deeper than your chest,
shoulders lowering without instruction,

a stomach without urgency,
stillness without self-monitoring,
rest without guilt.

For women who never learned safety early, these sensations can feel unfamiliar — even threatening. New does not always feel good at first. New feels uncertain.

And your nervous system does not trust new until it is shown — repeatedly — that nothing bad follows.

A GROUNDING MOMENT — LEARNING THE DIFFERENCE BETWEEN PAST AND PRESENT

There was a season when the smallest shift —
a delayed response, a quiet tone —
would send my body into alarm.

Heat. Tightness. Catastrophe.

But nothing was happening.

The realization came gently:
My body wasn't reacting to now.
It was reacting to memory.

And what it needed wasn't analysis —
it needed leadership.

The adult me had to step in and teach the difference.

SOFTENING THE HYPERVIGILANT CREATIVE

Softening is not weakness.
It is not surrender.
It is not naïveté.

Softening is the decision to stop rehearsing danger.

It does not erase discernment —
it frees discernment from fear.

This is the bridge between survival and presence,
between vigilance and creativity,
between who you had to be and who you are becoming.

Like all bridges, it must be crossed slowly.

WHAT NERVOUS SYSTEM SAFETY LOOKS LIKE IN REAL LIFE

Safety is not a routine or aesthetic.

It is a relationship.

It sounds like:

"I'm noticing tension — I'm going to pause."

"I don't feel safe — let me check whether this is memory or reality."

"I can slow down without something collapsing."

"I don't need to explain myself to earn ease."

Safety is not perfection.

Safety is permission.

FROM BRACING TO BREATHING (AN INVITATION)

Not steps — invitations.

Awareness.

Naming.

Discerning.

Offering safety.

Staying present.

Repeating.

Safety is learned the same way danger was learned — through repetition.

This is reparenting at a biological level.

WHAT CHANGES WHEN THE BODY FEELS SAFE

When hypervigilance softens, something quiet but profound happens.

Creativity widens.

Intuition clarifies.

Rest restores instead of numbs.

Boundaries become embodied.

A regulated creative woman is not less powerful — she is sustainable.

She moves from center, not alarm.

CLOSING REFLECTION — RETURNING TO INNER QUIET

Your hypervigilance was not a failure.
It was love in the only language your body knew.

But you are not living there anymore.

Your life is different now.
Your world is broader.
Your nervous system is ready for a new rhythm.

This chapter is your invitation back to inner quiet —
not emptiness,
but the quiet where creativity breathes,
where safety settles,
where the body finally unclenches.

You are not learning to be less alert.
You are learning to be more alive.

And in the next chapter, we turn toward the companion to safety:
rest, rhythm, and enoughness —
not as tasks to complete,
but as the natural language of a woman who no longer has to brace
for her life.

CHAPTER 14 -
Relearning Rest, Routine
& Enoughness

How to Create a Life Your Body Doesn't Have to Recover From
Once a hypervigilant creative woman begins to soften, something unexpected happens.

Her body doesn't immediately feel relief.

It feels confused.

You would think safety would feel natural—but for women who learned to live in emotional survival, safety feels unfamiliar. Quiet feels suspicious. Stillness feels like standing in an empty room with the lights off.

Your nervous system may finally be loosening its grip, but it hasn't yet learned to trust the calm.

This is why, right after hypervigilance softens, your oldest patterns tend to resurface. The urge to stay busy. The discomfort with slowing down. The subtle guilt that creeps in when you aren't being useful or productive. The panic that arises when there's nothing demanding your attention.

Slowness can feel like regression.

Stillness can feel like exposure.

Rest can feel like falling behind.

But none of this is failure.

This is the aftershock of safety—the moment your body encounters a life where danger no longer dictates the pace, and doesn't yet know how to respond.

This chapter is where that response is learned.

Where rest becomes safety.

Where routine becomes self-mothering.

Where enoughness becomes the emotional home your younger self never had.

WHY REST NEVER FELT RESTFUL

Rest feels complicated when you grow up inside emotional unpredictability.

As a child, rest often came with risk. Stillness meant exposure. Quiet carried tension. Slowing down felt like losing ground. Worth was tied to usefulness, alertness, performance—never presence.

So you learned to stay moving.

Not because ambition drove you, but because fear never stopped chasing you.

A hypervigilant creative woman does not fear work.

She fears the moment work stops—because that's when everything she outran has space to surface.

Which is why rest has always felt like too much.

And also why rest is the doorway into your becoming.

A body raised in chaos doesn't soften when it's tired—it accelerates.

A body shaped by criticism doesn't relax in safety—it braces.

A body formed in neglect doesn't unwind in stillness—it panics.

This is not a personal failing.

It's conditioning.

Your nervous system isn't rejecting rest because you lack discipline.

It's rejecting rest because it doesn't recognize it.

Rest is a language your body was never taught.

This chapter is where you begin teaching it.

WHEN STILLNESS FINALLY ARRIVED

There was a season in my life when I stayed in motion constantly—creating, achieving, building—because slowing down felt like stepping into a void.

I called it ambition.

I told myself I was disciplined.

I believed I was simply committed to my growth.

But beneath all of it was a quieter truth:

I was afraid of what I would feel if I stopped.

Afraid of the loneliness.

Afraid of the ache.

Afraid the silence would uncover the parts of myself I had buried beneath productivity.

The first time I truly rested—rested without distraction, without justification—my body shook.

Not from exhaustion.

From release.

That was the moment I realized something that changed everything:

My fatigue didn't come from overworking.

It came from over-bracing.

Rest wasn't the absence of activity.

Rest was the absence of fear.

REST AS THE FIRST SIGNAL OF SAFETY

True rest does not numb the nervous system.

It recalibrates it.

It doesn't pull you out of your body.

It brings you back into it.

Rest, in this season, doesn't ask you to disappear.

It asks you to arrive.

At first, this kind of rest is subtle.

It might look like letting your shoulders drop without correcting your posture.

Allowing your breath to deepen without monitoring it.

Sitting in silence for a few minutes without reaching for a screen.

These moments are not indulgent.

They are instructive.

Each one teaches your body a new truth:

Nothing bad is happening right now.

You don't need to brace.

You are allowed to be here.

This is how safety is learned—not through insight, but through repetition.

ROUTINE: THE STRUCTURE YOUR INNER CHILD NEVER HAD

Many creative women resist routine because they were taught that structure limits freedom.

But for the woman shaped by a mother wound, routine isn't restriction.

Routine is relief.

Routine says: *You won't be blindsided today.*

You won't have to improvise your emotional survival.

You know what comes next.

Where chaos once ruled, predictability begins to settle the body.

This doesn't mean rigid schedules or perfection.

It means anchors—small, dependable rhythms your nervous system can rely on.

A consistent morning check-in with yourself.

A regular moment of nourishment.

A predictable wind-down at night.

Routine becomes the quiet proof that someone is paying attention now.

Someone is tracking your needs.

Someone is protecting your energy.

That someone is you.

This is not discipline as force.

This is discipline as care.

ENOUGHNESS: THE IDENTITY SHIFT THAT CHANGES EVERYTHING

For many creative women raised in emotional neglect, the hardest lesson is this:

Enoughness was never modeled.

It was always conditional.

You learned you were enough when you were achieving, producing, pleasing, or excelling.

You learned you were not enough when you rested, paused, asked for help, or simply existed without output.

So adulthood inherited the same rules.

Enoughness, then, is not something you *believe* your way into.

It's something you *practice* your way toward.

Enoughness sounds like a new internal language:

"I've done enough for today."

"I don't have to earn rest."

"My worth is not a negotiation."

"I can move slowly and still be progressing."

"I am not behind. I am becoming."

These are not affirmations.

They are acts of reparenting.

Every time you choose rest without guilt, routine without rigidity, and presence without performance, your body learns what your childhood never taught it:

You are safe even when you are not proving anything.

A LIFE THAT NO LONGER REQUIRES RECOVERY

A rested creative woman is not diminished.

She is clarified.

When rest, routine, and enoughness take root, something stabilizes.

Your intuition sharpens because it's no longer competing with fear.

Your creativity deepens because it's no longer fueled by urgency.

Your energy becomes sustainable because it isn't constantly leaking through vigilance.

You stop needing to recover from your own life.

Not because the world became easier—

but because your body finally trusts you.

CLOSING REFLECTION — MAKING PEACE A PLACE YOU CAN LIVE

Your mother may not have known how to rest.

She may not have known how to slow down.

She may not have known how to feel like enough.

But you are learning now.

You are building a life your younger self would have felt safe inside—

a life that doesn't demand bracing, exhaustion, or constant proving.

A life that feels like home not because the world changed,

but because you did.

And in the next chapter, we turn toward reclamation:

how creativity, purpose, and vision rise differently when they are born from nervous system safety rather than survival.

Because from this place—

rested, rooted, and enough—

you no longer create to escape.

You create to live.

CHAPTER 15 - Rebirth & The Creative Awakening

The Return of Your True Self After Surviving the Mother Wound Healing has a rhythm you don't notice until you're already inside it.

First, your body begins to soften.

Then your breath deepens.

Then your nervous system stops bracing for impact.

And when the internal noise quiets enough for you to finally hear yourself, something almost imperceptible begins to shift.

Not dramatically.

Not all at once.

Not in a way anyone else could point to.

It happens softly—the way morning light enters a dark room before you realize it's day.

This is where rebirth begins.

Rebirth does not arrive because you demanded change or reached a finish line.

Rebirth arrives because, for the first time, there is enough internal safety for your real self to surface.

Your nervous system is no longer in constant defense.

Your routines are beginning to nourish instead of deplete you.

Your body trusts you more than it ever has.

And in that new quiet, your spirit finally has room to speak.

THE FIRST WHISPER OF REBIRTH

Rebirth rarely announces itself with clarity.

It enters as a noticing.

A slight discomfort with what used to feel normal.

A quiet resistance to environments you once tolerated.

A subtle tug toward something you cannot yet name.

You begin to sense that the life you've been living no longer fits—not because it was wrong, but because you are growing past it.

Rebirth is not a moment.

It is an awareness.

An awareness that the woman you learned to be in order to survive is no longer the woman you can continue to be.

An awareness that survival is no longer your primary language.

An awareness that something inside you is stretching, testing its edges, asking:

What if I didn't have to live like this anymore?

This is how the creative awakening begins—

not in chaos,

not in collapse,

but in the quiet that arrives after the nervous system stops screaming.

THE DEATH THAT MAKES REBIRTH POSSIBLE

Every rebirth is preceded by a death—but not the kind people usually imagine.

Not the death of a relationship.

Not the death of your mother.

Not even the death of an old identity.

The real death is quieter and more precise.

It is the death of the fantasy.

The fantasy that one day she would change.

That she would soften.

That she would finally see you.

That your patience, goodness, or worthiness could draw warmth out of her distance.

This fantasy was not foolish—it was protective.

It was how the child inside you survived.

But rebirth begins when your spirit can no longer carry false hope in one hand and your becoming in the other.

You don't release the fantasy in bitterness or rage.

You release it because something truer is asking to live.

And when the fantasy dies, space opens.

Space for your voice.

Space for your truth.

Space for the woman you are becoming.

You stop organizing your life around who she wasn't.

And you begin discovering who you are.

THE MOMENT YOU BEGIN TO HEAR YOURSELF

Rebirth often reveals itself in ordinary moments—

washing dishes,

sitting in traffic,

walking to your car,

lying awake when the house is finally still.

And then you hear it.

Clear.

Steady.

Undeniable.

I can't live like this anymore.

The voice isn't dramatic.

It isn't panicked.

It isn't loud.

It's honest.

This is the moment your true self speaks louder than your inherited conditioning.

It is psychological, spiritual, and somatic all at once.

The nervous system releasing what it can no longer sustain.

The inner child loosening patterns she once needed.

The adult self stepping forward to take the lead.

This is the inner turning.

The quiet revolt.

The beginning of your becoming.

THE CREATIVE SELF STIRS FIRST

Creative women feel rebirth before they understand it.

Because creativity is the part of you that has always known the truth.

Before your language changes, creativity responds.

Before your behavior shifts, creativity signals.

Before your life rearranges, creativity knocks.

Ideas start arriving that feel too large for the version of you that existed last year.

Desires surface that no longer shrink themselves to be acceptable.

Imaginings appear that refuse to fit inside old roles.

Creativity whispers:

There is a version of you waiting on the other side of your fear.

This is not coincidence. Creativity does not simply return during rebirth—it leads it.

Your art introduces you to the woman you are becoming long before the world catches up.

This is why the creative awakening feels both exhilarating and disorienting:

your inner world expands first.

LEAVING THE OLD WORLD (WITHOUT EVER PACKING A BAG)

Leaving the old world is not always literal.

Some women leave cities.

Some leave belief systems.

Some leave silence.

Some leave emotional roles built entirely on survival.

But all women in rebirth leave something.

Because rebirth is impossible inside the same emotional ecosystem that required your shrinking.

The old world is not a place.

It is a posture.

A pattern.

A psychology.

Leaving it means you stop negotiating for crumbs of validation. It means you become unavailable for emotional environments that mirror your childhood.

It means you no longer mistake endurance for love.

You didn't become cold.

You became finished with self-abandonment.

This is the migration—from survival to selfhood.

THE QUIET LONELINESS OF BECOMING

Rebirth often carries a loneliness—not because you are alone, but because you are no longer who you were.

You are not missing people.

You are outgrowing roles.

This loneliness is not a punishment.

It is a corridor.

A passage between the woman you were and the woman you are becoming.

In this space, something steadies.

Your intuition sharpens.

Your boundaries root.

Your creativity expands without apology.

You begin drawing people who recognize you without needing you to disappear.

Loneliness gives way to resonance.

WHEN DOUBT APPEARS

Every rebirth is tested.

You will wonder if you imagined the harm.

If you should go back.

If you are allowed to choose this new life.

This doubt is not regression.

It is your nervous system checking the ground beneath you.

Rebirth becomes real the moment you choose yourself anyway—

not because fear is gone,

but because you refuse to abandon yourself again.

This is not collapse.

It is anchoring.

CLOSING REFLECTION — YOU ARE EMERGING

Rebirth is not reinvention.

It is not erasure.

It is not becoming "better."

It is becoming *undistorted*.

You are shedding roles survival forced you into.

You are releasing identities built from scarcity.

You are reclaiming parts of yourself that never disappeared—only waited.

Your creativity is expanding.

Your intuition is strengthening.

Your presence is deepening.

You are not becoming someone new.

You are becoming someone true.

And in the next chapter, we turn toward what comes after rebirth—

the reconstruction, the identity reshaping, the quiet strength required to live from this new center.

You are emerging.

And nothing in your old life can hold you anymore.

CHAPTER 16 - The Reinvention

How the Woman You Were Meant to Become Begins to Emerge
By the time you reach this point, something inside you is already different.

You may not be able to name it yet—but you can feel it.

After rebirth, there is often a strange in-between:
You are no longer who you were,
but you are not yet sure who you are becoming.

Nothing is wrong with you in this space.
This is what transition feels like when it is real.

Rebirth is the inner awakening—the soft return to yourself.
Reinvention is what follows when that awakening begins asking for form.

If the previous chapter was the quiet stirring—the breath, the recognition, the internal shift—
this chapter is where your life starts responding.

Reinvention is not force.
It is not reinvention as performance or reinvention as escape.

It is what happens when your inner safety becomes strong enough for your outer life to stop pretending.

WHEN THE UNFINISHED SELF FINALLY GETS TO GROW

Many creative women quietly believe they are late.

Late to clarity.

Late to confidence.

Late to purpose.

Late to themselves.

But you were never late.

You were unmodeled.

You were asked to become a woman without emotional scaffolding.

To form identity without mirrors.

To mature inside a house where growth was not supported.

So you improvised.

You learned adulthood the way self-taught artists learn technique—

by watching, feeling, guessing, experimenting.

You learned through contrast instead of guidance.

This did not make you underdeveloped.

It made you intuitive.

It made you adaptive.

It made you deeply perceptive.

Reinvention begins the moment you stop framing your life as failure

and start seeing it as preparation.

HOW REINVENTION ACTUALLY BEGINS

Reinvention does not begin with a decision.

It begins with discomfort.

A subtle restlessness.

A quiet resistance to what once felt acceptable.

A growing sense that something no longer fits—even if you can't explain why.

You might notice:

- your tolerance shrinking

- your body resisting old environments
- your creativity pushing against familiar containers
- your spirit pulling forward while fear lingers behind

This is not impulsiveness.

This is readiness.

When safety enters the nervous system, truth follows.

Reinvention is the moment survival stops being impressive enough

to justify staying small.

WHAT ONCE FELT LIKE DETOURS REVEALS ITSELF AS TRAINING

Before reinvention takes shape, your life often looks scattered.

The wrong jobs.

The misaligned relationships.

The creative collaborations that drained instead of fed you.

The communities where you felt almost—but not fully—at home.

At the time, it looked like confusion.

In hindsight, it becomes clear:

Each environment taught you what your spirit could not hold.

Each disappointment refined your discernment.

Each misfit sharpened your intuition.

Creative women often learn through lived experience what others learn through modeling.

Pain became curriculum.

Contrast became clarity.

Nothing was wasted.

WHEN THE CREATIVE SELF RETURNS TO LEAD

Every creative woman carries two internal identities:

The artist she was born as

and the child she had to become to survive.

Reinvention is the moment those two no longer compete.

Your creativity stops functioning as armor
and starts acting as direction.

You notice it when:

- ideas feel too alive for the life you're living
- your voice deepens without effort
- your work feels less performative and more honest

You are no longer creating to escape yourself. You are creating to express yourself.

This is alignment—not ambition. Your creativity is no longer compensating for neglect. It is responding to safety.

STEPPING INTO A WOMAN YOU WERE NEVER SHOWN

Reinvention is awkward.

No one prepares you for that part.

You are stepping into a version of womanhood your lineage never modeled:

a woman who trusts herself,

a woman who belongs to herself,

a woman led by internal truth instead of emotional survival.

At first, you may feel unsure.

That does not mean you are unready.

It means you are early.

You will practice speaking differently.

You will set boundaries without knowing if they'll be respected.

You will choose rest where you once chose rescue.

You will let desire take up space before confidence arrives.

Identity is not built through certainty.

It is built through staying.

And slowly—almost imperceptibly—you stop shrinking in rooms.

You stop adjusting to survive.

You begin expanding to meet your life.

That is reinvention.

HOW CALLING EMERGES FROM BECOMING

A creative calling does not arrive before reinvention.
It arrives because of it.

Your calling clarifies as your nervous system stabilizes.
Your direction sharpens as your self-trust deepens.

You stop creating to explain yourself.
You start creating because something true is moving through you.

Your work gains weight—not because you tried harder,
but because you are no longer fragmented.

Calling is not a fantasy.
Calling is coherence.

It is the life that becomes possible
when survival is no longer running the show.

CLOSING REFLECTION — THE FORM OF YOUR FUTURE

Reinvention is not a single moment.
It is an unfolding.

A gradual restructuring where the woman who once adapted
makes room for the woman who can now lead.

You are not reinventing because you failed.
You are reinventing because you finally have the safety to grow.

And now—
as you stand inside this becoming—
the next chapter moves you forward again:

How to build a creative life, body of work, and sense of purpose
from sovereignty instead of survival.

You are no longer improvising your life.
You are shaping it.

And the world is ready for the woman you are finally allowing
yourself to be.

CHAPTER 17 - You are Arriving On Time

Why Your Timeline Is Not Delayed — It Is Custom, Compassionate, and Perfectly Aligned With Your Becoming

There is a quiet fear many creative women raised without emotional safety carry long after the worst is over.

It isn't dramatic.

It doesn't announce itself loudly.

It lives beneath ambition, beneath healing, beneath even hope.

What if I waited too long?

What if I missed my life?

It surfaces in moments of comparison, in pauses between chapters, in the stillness after survival finally loosens its grip. You lie awake not in crisis, but in wondering:

If I had been loved differently... would I be further by now?

Let me answer you clearly — and calmly — without urgency or persuasion:

You are not late.

You are not behind.

You did not miss your moment.

You are arriving in the first season of your life where your spirit finally has the safety required to grow.

What most women mistake for lateness is actually recovery.
What looks like delay is often protection.
And healing doesn't pause the timeline — it reshapes it.

You Were Not Late — You Were Unseen

Women who grow up without emotional support do not begin at the same starting line.

Before you ever explored your creativity, you were already working.
Before you ever dreamed freely, you were already managing.
Before you ever felt entitled to desire, you were already surviving.

You were learning how to read moods.
How to anticipate silence.
How to regulate yourself without guidance.
How to become an adult without mirrors.

Your peers were not ahead of you.
They were simply not carrying what you were carrying.

What looked like "lost time" was actually invisible labor — emotional, psychological, somatic work no one applauded and no one taught.

Creativity doesn't disappear under that weight.
It waits.

The Years You Thought You Were Behind

There was a long stretch of my life where I felt perpetually ten years late.

Not metaphorically — literally.

I entered adulthood without a blueprint. I learned life by improvisation, by observation, by trial and error. I longed to be the woman I could feel inside myself, but there was a gulf between potential and embodiment — a gap no one had taught me how to cross.

For a long time, I believed that if my mother had supported me — if she had nurtured my creativity, my confidence, my voice — I would have arrived earlier.

But here is the truth I couldn't see back then:

Had opportunity come before safety, I would not have survived it.

My boundaries were too thin.

My self-trust too fragile.

My giving too unchecked.

The very things that delayed my arrival were the things that saved me from collapse.

What I once called delay, I now recognize as protection.

Healing Doesn't Slow You Down — It Prepares You

Women with mother wounds often enter adulthood without something foundational:

Safety.

Before you could explore, your nervous system had to stabilize.

Before you could create freely, your body had to learn trust.

Before you could sustain visibility, your system had to learn regulation.

Creativity cannot bloom inside vigilance.

Vision cannot expand inside fear.

So yes — your creative life may have opened later.

Not because you lacked ambition.

But because your body needed safety before expression.

That is not failure.

That is wisdom.

The Exhaustion Isn't Proof You Should Stop

Many women misread their exhaustion.

They assume it means they're failing, falling behind, incapable of keeping up.

But what you're experiencing is something far more specific:

You are building a future while still tending to a past that never had care.

You are rising while dismantling old emotional ruins.

That is not weakness.

That is transition.

You're not keeping up with others.

You're finally catching up with yourself.

Returning "Late" Makes You Deeper, Not Lesser

Some women whisper to themselves:

I'm rusty.

I should have started earlier.

Everyone else is ahead.

But a delayed beginning is not a diminished one.

You don't return to your creativity as the girl who left it behind.

You return as the woman who lived.

And that woman carries discernment.

She carries emotional accuracy.

She carries depth.

She carries truth.

Youth gives creativity energy.

Life gives creativity weight.

And weight is what makes art unforgettable.

Readiness Does Not Feel the Way You Expected

Most people think readiness feels like confidence.

It doesn't.

Readiness sounds like:

I'm scared — but I'm not trapped.

I don't know the path — but I know I'm not going back.

Readiness is not the absence of fear.

It is the presence of capacity.

Your life did not withhold opportunity from you.

It waited until you could hold it.

You Cannot Miss What Is Meant for Your Capacity

Your calling is not age-based.

It is capacity-based.

Visibility requires grounding.

Opportunity requires regulation.

Success requires an internal home to return to.

What has not arrived yet was not withheld — it was being protected.

Your destiny does not operate on a clock.

It responds to nervous system readiness.

And now — for the first time — your system is ready.

You Are Arriving, Exactly On Time

You did not take the long way.

You took the necessary one.

Every pause shaped your discernment.

Every delay strengthened your foundation.

Every detour refined your voice.

Your gift did not leave you behind.

It waited — until you had a life stable enough to hold it.

And now, as you stand here — clearer, steadier, embodied — you are not late to your life.

You are right on schedule.

For the first time in your becoming,

you are arriving

exactly when you were meant to.

CHAPTER 18 - Your Voice Matters

Returning to the Sound of Yourself After a Lifetime of Shrinking There is a moment in healing when silence begins to loosen its grip.

Not suddenly.

Not dramatically.

But gently — almost shyly.

It happens in small ways at first.

A sentence you don't rewrite three times.

A thought you say out loud before fear has time to edit it.

A boundary that leaves your mouth without the familiar trembling.

Something inside you begins to move.

Not the voice that learned to perform in order to stay safe.

Not the voice that smoothed over discomfort to keep connection intact.

Not the voice that tiptoed around other people's capacity.

Your voice — the one that existed before you learned to contort it.

This chapter is not about reclaiming something you lost.

It is about recognizing what survived.

Because your voice never disappeared.

It learned how to hide.

THE VOICE THAT LEARNED TO WAIT

For years, your voice adapted to the emotional environments around you.

It became measured.

Careful.

Appropriate.

You learned when to speak — and when not to.

You learned which truths were welcome — and which ones made people withdraw.

You learned how to soften your edges before anyone had the chance to punish them.

That wasn't weakness.

That was intelligence.

But the voice you are meeting now sounds different.

It no longer asks permission to exist.

It no longer minimizes its needs to keep peace.

It no longer abandons itself mid-sentence.

It no longer disappears to protect someone else's comfort.

Your voice is not returning because you suddenly became brave.

It is returning because you are finally safe.

Safety — not confidence — is where expression begins.

HOW VOICE ACTUALLY RETURNS

Many women expect their voice to come back all at once — loud, bold, undeniable.

But voice doesn't return like a breakthrough.

It returns like a sequence.

It begins with preference.

Small, quiet statements that orient you back to yourself:

"I don't want that."

"I do want this."

"I'm tired."

"I'm ready."

Preference is identity's first language.

Before you declare who you are, you begin by naming what you want.

From preference grows truth.

This is the voice that carries clarity and direction:

"That hurt."

"That dynamic no longer works for me."

"I won't participate in this anymore."

"I need something else."

Truth isn't confrontation.

Truth is orientation.

It tells you which way to turn.

And once truth has roots, expression becomes natural.

Your voice begins showing up in your writing.

In your art.

In your boundaries.

In your leadership.

In your presence.

At this stage, voice stops performing.

It starts inhabiting.

WHAT A MUTED VOICE COSTS A CREATIVE WOMAN

Creatives do not lose their voice quietly.

When expression is suppressed, creativity collapses inward.

Intuition dulls.

Risk-taking shrinks.

Originality flattens.

Ideas lose their urgency.

Your inner world feels full — but unheard.

A muted voice creates a muted life.

And nothing aches a creative woman more than sensing the fullness of who she is

without hearing it reflected in her own words.

Voice is not an accessory.

Voice is oxygen.

WHY YOUR VOICE IS POSSIBLE NOW

Your voice isn't emerging because you forced it.
It's emerging because:

- your boundaries are working
- your nervous system is softening
- your adult self is present
- your inner child no longer has to testify alone

Voice grows where safety exists.
And the safety you have now — you built it.
Slowly.
Intentionally.
Choice by choice.

This is the first time in your life where your voice doesn't just *want* to emerge.

It *can*.

A MOMENT FROM MY OWN LIFE

There came a point in my healing when silence no longer felt protective.
It felt like withholding.

Not from other people — from myself.

I realized that if I didn't speak about what I had lived through, another creative woman might stay trapped in a cycle she didn't yet have language for.

So I started writing.

Not because I felt fearless.
Not because I felt qualified.
But because I felt responsible — in the most grounded, human way — to break a loop that had already taken too much.

Using my voice wasn't about being loud.
It was about being honest.

And if my honesty could help even one woman recognize herself sooner,

then my voice mattered — even if it shook.

Yours does too.

IF YOU CAN'T HEAR YOUR VOICE YET

There is nothing wrong with you.

Some women have spent so long silencing themselves
that the first sound their voice makes is hesitation.

Voice returns quietly:

In a text you don't over-edit.

In a "no" you whisper.

In a creative idea you don't immediately dismiss.

In a truth you don't swallow.

In a boundary you don't walk back.

In a choice that surprises even you.

Your voice is not volume.

Your voice is direction.

THE WOMAN WHO SPEAKS NOW

Your voice is no longer a child pleading to be heard.

It belongs to:

- the woman who sets boundaries
- the woman who signs her name on her work
- the woman who walks away from misalignment
- the woman who no longer negotiates her truth
- the woman who can hold herself when she speaks

This is the voice that leads you forward.

CLOSING REFLECTION — YOUR VOICE IS YOUR RETURN

You were never waiting for permission.

You were waiting for safety.

And now that you've created that safety within yourself,
your voice rises — not as rebellion, not as defiance —
but as recognition.

"I am here.
I matter.
And I will no longer disappear in my own life."

Your voice is not something you reclaim.
It is something you *come home to.*

The world doesn't need you louder.
The world needs you *true.*

And for the first time,
you are healed enough
to sound like yourself.

CHAPTER 19 - Redefining Family, Love & Support

Belonging Without Shrinking

When your voice begins to return—when you start hearing yourself after years of editing, softening, and swallowing—something quietly revealing happens.

You notice where your voice disappears.

Not everywhere.

Not all the time.

Just in certain rooms.

With certain people.

Inside certain dynamics that once felt familiar, even comforting.

You catch yourself going quiet without deciding to.

Bracing without knowing why.

Shrinking mid-sentence the way you used to.

This noticing is not regression.

It is clarity.

And it marks the moment you begin redefining family—not as the people who share your history, but as the people who can witness your becoming without requiring your disappearance.

For creative women raised without emotional safety, this realization rarely arrives with celebration. It arrives with gravity. With courage. With the understanding that belonging is no longer something you chase—it is something you choose.

This chapter is not about replacing your mother.

It is not about cutting people off.

It is not about bitterness, rebellion, or building a fantasy version of "new family."

It is about sovereignty.

It is about claiming the authority to decide who gets proximity to your inner world now that you have one.

Because for the first time in your life, you are no longer choosing connection through survival.

You are choosing it through truth.

Family Is an Emotional Climate, Not a Bloodline

You were taught that family is inherited.

But your body learned something else.

Family is the emotional climate you live inside.

It is the atmosphere your nervous system breathes.

The tone you don't have to manage.

The space where your creativity doesn't have to apologize for existing.

True belonging feels like a place where your body softens instead of braces, where you don't perform to stay included, where your sensitivity isn't treated as a liability, and where growth isn't met with punishment or withdrawal.

If this was not your experience growing up, nothing about you failed.

What failed was the environment's ability to offer safety.

And here is the truth you are finally ready to live inside:

belonging is not a blood contract—it is an emotional alignment.

Your lineage shaped your beginning.

But you now get to decide your climate.

Why Creative Women Need Different Kinds of Support

Creative women don't just feel—they translate.

You absorb the emotional frequency of rooms.

You register what isn't said.

You create from atmosphere as much as intention.

This sensitivity was never weakness.

It was your instrument.

But growing up in emotional unpredictability taught you to internalize everything—to manage moods, anticipate rupture, and create inner worlds because the outer one had no room for you.

Your creativity survived because you turned inward.

But that survival strategy came at a cost.

Sometimes the shift begins not with insight—but with contrast.

For me, it happened after moving to Los Angeles.

Coming from an environment where people hid the parts of themselves they feared would be judged, I didn't realize how heavy that emotional climate had been until I stepped into one that felt different.

Here, I saw people inhabiting their lives—not explaining them away. Communities formed around identity, creativity, expression, joy. I attended a simple all-women's gathering—nothing curated, nothing performative—and felt something I hadn't felt before.

My guard dropped without effort.

I wasn't scanning the room.

I wasn't managing tone.

I wasn't shrinking to maintain peace.

I was just… there.

Not because the women were "my new family."

But because the emotional climate finally matched who I was becoming.

That night taught me something fundamental:

Some environments shrink you.

Others free you.

Creative women do not thrive just anywhere.

They require spaces where the inner world is allowed to breathe.

This is why redefining family is not optional.

It is foundational.

Support Begins Inside—and Moves Outward

Most people believe support starts with other people.

But for the creative woman healing from a mother wound, support begins somewhere quieter.

It begins with becoming someone you belong to.

When you speak to yourself with dignity.

When you honor your limits instead of overriding them.

When you stop abandoning yourself for connection.

When you believe what you feel the first time.

From there, support extends outward—to the environments you inhabit.

Spaces shape you before people do.

Noise or calm. Chaos or rhythm. Pressure or permission.

You didn't leave your mother's emotional climate because you were disloyal.

You left because your nervous system could not grow there.

And only after that—only once you are rooted inside yourself and supported by your surroundings—do relationships become safe to choose.

Not because they promise intensity.

But because they allow consistency.

Real support does not demand your contraction.

It does not punish your boundaries.

It does not ask you to remain who you were to keep love.

Belonging that costs you yourself is not belonging.

It is reenactment.

The Quiet Season That Often Follows

When women redefine family, a quieter season often arrives.

Not abandonment.

Not punishment.

A clearing.

A period where the noise falls away so your identity can stabilize.

In this space, boundaries take root.

Discernment sharpens.

Creativity returns without apology.

You are not losing people.

You are losing access to versions of yourself you can no longer afford to be.

This is not loneliness.

It is preparation.

How You Know a Space Is Safe

Safety is not theoretical.

It is physiological.

You know you are aligned when your body does not brace for entry, when your breath deepens without permission, when your voice doesn't disappear mid-thought.

You know a relationship is safe when your growth is welcomed instead of threatened, when your boundaries land without backlash, when reciprocity exists without negotiation.

These are not luxuries.

They are prerequisites.

You are not asking for too much.

You are finally asking for the right things.

The Truth About "Soul Family"

You don't find soul family.

You become the woman they can recognize.

They arrive when you stop performing, stop rescuing, stop confusing chaos with connection, and stop offering discounts on your presence.

They do not replace your mother.

They do not heal the wound.

They simply do not ask you to bleed for belonging.

And that changes everything.

Support Is Emotional Alignment

Support is not someone who stays.

Support is someone whose presence does not cost you yourself.

It feels like room to expand.

Permission to rest.

Encouragement without pressure.

Boundaries without punishment.

Love without erasure.

Support is not emotional labor.

Support is emotional alignment.

CLOSING REFLECTION — BEGINNING AGAIN

Redefining family is not betrayal.

It is emotional leadership.

You are not rejecting your lineage.

You are refining it.

You are not becoming cold.

You are becoming clear.

You are not ending belonging.

You are beginning it—on terms that honor your nervous system, your creativity, and your truth.

Family is no longer something you inherit.

It is something you build.

And you begin building it the moment you decide:

"I will never again stay where I have to disappear."

In the next chapter, you step into the rooms your healing has prepared you for—spaces where your voice can rise, your creativity can deepen, and your identity can stand without bracing.

You are not redefining family.

You are redefining home.

CHAPTER 20 - Entering New Rooms

Standing in Bigger Spaces Without Shrinking, Performing, or Asking for Permission

By the time you reach this stage of healing, something subtle has already changed.

You don't fear visibility the way you once did.

You no longer believe you must disappear to stay safe.

And still—when life begins to open doors your childhood never prepared you for, you may feel the quiet tremor beneath your feet.

Not panic.

Not doubt.

Just the unfamiliar sensation of standing somewhere new **without bracing**.

This chapter isn't about ambition or external success.

It's about capacity—the internal steadiness required to *inhabit* a bigger life without abandoning yourself inside it.

Readiness is not confidence.

It's not certainty.

It's not perfection.

Readiness is regulation.

The ability to remain present, grounded, and intact while being seen.

And now—perhaps for the first time—you are healed enough to enter rooms you once survived by shrinking.

When the Room Feels Bigger—but You Don't Collapse

There are rooms your spirit recognized long before your nervous system felt ready to stand inside them.

Rooms aligned with your becoming long before you believed you were allowed to enter.

Rooms you once imagined from a distance, assuming they belonged to *other* women—women who were louder, steadier, less wounded.

But the truth is simpler:

Those rooms weren't intimidating.

You just weren't regulated enough to stay inside them yet.

Healing doesn't make rooms appear.

Healing makes rooms sustainable.

A Moment From My Own Becoming

When I moved to Los Angeles, I didn't realize I was walking into one of the first rooms my healed self could finally handle.

Nobody here knew who I had been.

No one knew the girl who softened herself to keep the peace.

No one expected me to explain my history or minimize my presence.

LA only saw the woman who walked into the room.

And something in my body noticed the difference immediately.

I wasn't scanning faces.

I wasn't editing my words.

I wasn't bracing for who might feel threatened by my joy or ambition.

I felt present.

I felt grounded.

I felt... allowed.

That's when I understood something important:

Some rooms don't require courage.

They require capacity.

And the room hadn't changed.

I had.

The Rooms You Enter Always Mirror the Room Inside You

Creative women shaped by emotional neglect often learn one early lesson:

Visibility is dangerous.

Not because you lacked talent—but because your earliest environments taught you that being seen came with consequences.

Joy drew resentment.

Expression invited withdrawal.

Success disrupted the emotional balance.

Needs caused collapse.

So your body learned a strategy that once kept you safe:

Shrink—and you survive.

That adaptation may have protected the child you were.

But it quietly keeps the adult woman you are **outside rooms that were built for her**.

Here is the truth most women never hear:

You don't rise into bigger rooms.

You rise into a bigger internal capacity—and the room meets you there.

When Success Tests the Nervous System (Not the Talent)

Bigger rooms don't ask if you're worthy.

They ask if you can stay.

Stay present while being witnessed.

Stay grounded while being praised.

Stay yourself while attention lingers.

For women with mother wounds, this is the real edge—not the task, but the *witnessing*.

Your body remembers:

- the silence that followed your boldness
- the coldness that followed your success
- the tension that arrived when you needed support

So entering larger spaces isn't a career move.

It's a somatic expansion.

You're not learning how to be seen.

You're learning how to *remain*.

The Two Old Survival Postures (And Why They're No Longer Needed)

Before healing, most women carried one of two adaptations into visibility:

Some shrank.

They waited.

They minimized.

They hoped permission would arrive.

Others performed.

They overworked.

They overdelivered.

They stayed busy to stay safe.

Both were intelligent.

Both were protective.

Both were exhausting.

And neither are required anymore.

Regulation replaces both shrinking and performing.

Presence replaces permission.

What Readiness Actually Feels Like

Readiness is not loud.

It feels like:

- your shoulders staying relaxed when attention lands on you
- your voice remaining steady without rehearsal
- silence no longer registering as danger
- praise passing through without pressure
- misunderstanding not collapsing your center

You are not fearless.

You are present.

You are not invincible.

You are regulated.

This is what it means to be healed enough.

The Moment the Question Changes

At some point, the inner dialogue shifts.

Not:

"Do they think I belong here?"

But:

"Does this room align with who I'm becoming?"

When that question leads:

You choose environments differently.

You collaborate differently.

You walk away sooner.

You no longer fit yourself to rooms—rooms must fit *you*.

This is not arrogance.

This is adulthood.

This is leadership.

Why Timing Was Protection, Not Delay

Some rooms would have cost you too much earlier.

Not as punishment—but as protection.

Because entering too soon often leads to:

- shrinking instead of shining
- performing instead of expressing
- misreading neutrality as rejection
- mistaking feedback for identity
- abandoning yourself to belong

Healing didn't make you deserving of bigger rooms.

Healing made you *able to stay inside them*.

How You Know You're Ready

Not by confidence.

Not by certainty.

But by this:

You no longer leave parts of yourself at the door.

You no longer negotiate your worth for access.

You don't ask permission to exist.

You are not entering rooms to be chosen.

You are entering rooms because **you have chosen yourself**.

Closing Reflection — Standing Where You Once Would Have Disappeared

You don't enter bigger rooms to prove anything.

You enter them because your body no longer collapses under possibility.

Your past no longer dictates your posture.

Your nervous system no longer interprets opportunity as danger.

Your presence no longer trembles at expansion.

You are anchored enough to stand.

Regulated enough to stay.

Whole enough to rise.

This is not bravado.

This is arrival.

And for the first time in your life,

you are not stepping into rooms hoping to belong—

You belong because you are there.

CHAPTER 21 - Becoming The Leader Of Your Own Life

W here Healing Matures into Self-Trust, Direction, and Daily Autonomy

There comes a moment in healing that doesn't feel like a break-through —

it feels like a quiet rearrangement.

Nothing dramatic happens.

No emotional surge.

No declaration.

You simply notice that your past no longer grabs the steering wheel every time something unfamiliar appears.

The ache is still there — but it no longer pilots you.

The memories still exist — but they don't dictate your next move.

The people who shaped your earliest wounds may still appear in your story — but they no longer write the script.

This is the moment healing matures into leadership.

Not leadership as performance.

Not leadership as control.

Not leadership as independence forged from pain.

But leadership as *grounded authorship* — the embodied realization:

I can lead my life now.

Self-leadership doesn't announce itself.

It reveals itself through moments you almost miss.

The first time you tell the truth without rehearsing it.

The moment you enforce a boundary and your body doesn't flood with panic.

The day you stop consulting old survival instincts before making ordinary decisions.

The quiet shift where you begin asking yourself — not others — *What do I want to do next?*

This is not confidence.

This is orientation.

You are no longer waiting to be chosen, corrected, or directed.

You are no longer organizing your life around other people's limits.

You are beginning to trust yourself with yourself.

WHEN SURVIVAL STOPS MAKING DECISIONS FOR YOU

For women raised without emotional modeling, early adulthood often becomes an exercise in avoidance.

Avoiding disappointment.

Avoiding conflict.

Avoiding visibility.

Avoiding needs that were never welcomed.

Not because you were incapable —

but because survival trained you to reduce risk instead of expand possibility.

Self-leadership begins the moment that internal posture changes.

Not all at once.

Not heroically.

You simply stop outsourcing your authority to the past.

You start noticing:

I don't have to repeat this.

I don't have to tolerate that.

I don't have to stay confused.

Healing becomes directional.

You begin choosing from who you are becoming — not from who you once needed to be.

THE MOMENT SELF-ABANDONMENT ENDS

The deepest wound of the mother-wounded creative is not abandonment itself.

It is the *self-abandonment learned in response to it.*

Self-leadership is the moment that pattern quietly dissolves.

You stop negotiating your dreams to protect someone else's comfort.

You stop shrinking to keep rooms emotionally stable.

You stop waiting for a mother, mentor, partner, or authority figure to validate what you already know.

You no longer confuse peacekeeping with maturity.

You no longer mistake endurance for strength.

You no longer silence truth in exchange for belonging.

Instead, something steadier emerges:

I will not leave myself again.

This is not defiance.

This is adulthood.

A MOMENT FROM MY OWN LIFE

There was a time when I believed adulthood meant tolerating whatever people offered —

disrespect, inconsistency, broken commitments — because no one had ever shown me another option.

That belief stayed with me for years.

Not because it felt right — but because it felt familiar.

A few years ago, I was building something meaningful with a friend in business.

Plans. Momentum. Shared vision.

But behind the scenes, there were lies.

Diminishment.

Broken promises.

The old version of me would have rationalized it.

Worked harder.

Compensated.

Swallowed the discomfort to preserve the relationship.

But something had shifted.

One day — after another discovery that confirmed what my body already knew — a quiet clarity rose in me.

Not anger.

Not drama.

Just truth.

You don't have to accept this.

So I didn't.

I ended the partnership.

I took the loss.

I walked away.

And what surprised me most wasn't the fear —

it was the absence of regret.

Because once you realize you don't have to stay anywhere that shrinks you,

self-leadership stops being a concept and becomes a practice.

WHAT LEADERSHIP LOOKS LIKE IN A HEALED WOMAN

A self-led woman is not harsher.

She is clearer.

She is not colder.

She is steadier.

She does not rush — because she understands that what belongs to her cannot be missed.

She does not over-explain — because her decisions are rooted.

She does not need consensus — because she is no longer fragmented inside herself.

She makes choices that align with her nervous system.

She listens to resistance instead of overriding it.

She builds structures that support who she is becoming — not who she had to be.

She treats her creativity seriously.

Her rest intentionally.

Her boundaries as non-negotiable information.

This is not dominance.

This is self-trust matured into movement.

YOU WERE NOT WAITING FOR SOMEONE ELSE

As this identity settles — quietly, almost unremarkably — a realization lands:

You were never waiting for your mother to lead your life.

You were never waiting for permission to arrive.

You were never missing what you needed to begin.

You were waiting for *you*.

The version of you who could hold your own life without collapsing into old patterns.

The version of you who could make decisions without asking the past for approval.

The version of you who could stay present when things finally started working.

That woman is here now.

Leading not through force —

but through trust.

Leading not by erasing the past —

but by no longer letting it drive.

This is where healing becomes direction.

This is where awareness becomes authorship.

This is where your story stops orbiting the wound

and begins orbiting your becoming.

You are not learning how to lead your life.

You are finally doing it.

CHAPTER 22 - Where Survival Ends

Crossing the Threshold Into the Life You're Now Able to Live
There comes a moment in healing that doesn't feel dramatic or victorious — just unmistakable.

A moment when you realize you are no longer moving away from what hurt you.

You are moving toward yourself.

Nothing external announces this shift.

Your life may look mostly the same.

Your history hasn't vanished.

Your memories still exist.

But something fundamental has changed.

The past no longer functions as the compass you use to make decisions.

The ache still visits, but it no longer pilots your direction.

The people who shaped your earliest wounds still belong to your story — but they no longer author it.

It feels less like triumph and more like gravity resetting itself.

A quiet internal click.

Survival is no longer your operating system.

Selfhood has taken the lead.

This is not the end of healing.

This is the moment healing matures into authorship.

THE WOMAN READING THIS IS NOT THE WOMAN WHO BEGAN

Even if you cannot name it clearly yet, your internal landscape has reorganized.

You notice your patterns sooner.

You hesitate before abandoning yourself.

You recover faster when something stings.

You pause instead of spiraling.

You feel your voice returning — first in moments, then in instincts.

You no longer confuse intensity with truth.

You no longer confuse discomfort with danger.

You no longer need to collapse in order to feel safe again.

These shifts aren't emotional breakthroughs.

They are structural.

You have built an inner architecture that didn't exist before — one made of regulation, clarity, and the grounded maturity of a woman who is no longer steering her life from fear.

The woman who began this book was surviving.

The woman reading this chapter is integrating.

Your body knows it.

Your spirit knows it.

Your creativity knows it.

Something has crossed over.

THE FIRST TIME YOU CHOSE SELFHOOD WITHOUT DRAMA

For many women, the moment survival ends doesn't arrive in a crisis.

It arrives in a choice that no longer requires justification.

A boundary you enforce without rehearsing.

A departure you make without collapse.

A decision you stand inside without explaining yourself into exhaustion.

There may still be loss.

There may still be grief.

But there is no inner argument.

That's how you know.

Selfhood begins when you stop negotiating your dignity for belonging.

When the nervous system no longer flinches at self-respect.

When walking away feels cleaner than staying misaligned.

Not louder.

Not harder.

Just finished.

SURVIVAL WAS A STRATEGY — NOT AN IDENTITY

For much of your life, your nervous system organized itself around a single mandate:

Get through.

You anticipated moods that weren't yours.

You softened yourself to avoid rupture.

You overperformed to feel acceptable.

You stayed quiet to stay connected.

That wasn't weakness.

That was intelligence shaped by an unsafe environment.

But survival was never meant to become who you are.

It was a temporary solution to a problem you did not create.

And you outgrew it.

The fact that you can now choose truth over instinct, presence over performance, alignment over fear — without imploding — is evidence of selfhood.

You didn't come this far to recreate the emotional home that once required your disappearance.

You came this far to build something no one modeled for you:

A life shaped by clarity.

By emotional safety.

By self-respect.

By grounded identity.

By creative expression that no longer asks permission.

This is not rebellion.

This is adulthood.

FROM ESCAPING LIFE TO CREATING IT

When you grow up without emotional safety, imagination becomes refuge.

Your creativity wasn't avoidance — it was foresight.

Your inner world wasn't fantasy — it was rehearsal.

Something in you always knew another life was possible.

Now, creativity no longer functions as escape.

It becomes compass.

Leadership.

Expression.

You are no longer running from your life.

You are shaping it.

This is what it means to live from selfhood:

Not reacting to the past.

Not bracing for the future.

But choosing from the present with authority.

THE TRUE REWARD OF HEALING IS CAPACITY

Healing does not promise ease.

It promises space.

Capacity to stay regulated inside disappointment.

Capacity to be visible without shrinking.

Capacity to love with boundaries.

Capacity to speak without disappearing.

Capacity to walk away without collapse.

Capacity to rest without guilt.

Difficulty still exists.

But difficulty no longer becomes identity.

You are no longer the woman who turns rejection into truth.

Or exhaustion into self-definition.

Or proximity into proof of worth.

You are becoming the woman who knows:

"I am capable of supporting myself — emotionally, creatively, internally."

WHAT CHANGES FROM HERE

Because your inner structure has shifted, your outer life will respond.

You will notice misalignment sooner — and tolerate it less.

You will choose relationships shaped by reciprocity, not rescue.

You will speak with fewer words and more accuracy.

You will treat your creativity as calling, not coping.

You will rest because your body finally feels like home.

This is the quiet phase of healing no one warns you about — when your life begins to rise to meet the woman you've already become.

YOUR ART WILL CHANGE TOO

As survival loosens its grip, your voice sharpens.

Your intuition steadies.

Your expression deepens.

You no longer create to be chosen.

You create because you have chosen yourself.

Your art no longer tells the story of abandonment.

It reflects embodiment.

THIS IS THE THRESHOLD

Old patterns may still knock.

Grief may still visit.

Doubt may still whisper.

But none of it owns you anymore.

You know how to return to yourself now.

Healing didn't erase the past.

It removed its authority.

You are stepping into authorship.

Into selfhood.

Into a future that can finally hold you.

You are not behind.

You are not late.

You are not unfinished.

Survival is no longer your story.

Selfhood is.

And the life rising to meet you will not be shaped by the wound —
but by the woman who outgrew it.

CHAPTER 23 - The Practice Of Becoming

How You Live the Woman You've Worked So Hard to Heal
You didn't cross the threshold just to understand yourself. You crossed it to live differently.

In the last chapter, survival ended and selfhood began. That shift wasn't symbolic — it was structural. Something inside you reorganized. You stopped orienting your life around what hurt you and began orienting it around who you are.

And now comes the part few people prepare you for.

Not the breakthrough.

Not the realization.

Not the language.

The living.

This chapter is not about healing more.

It is about **inhabiting what has already healed**.

Because becoming yourself is not a moment you arrive at. It is a way you move through ordinary days without abandoning yourself inside them.

BECOMING IS NO LONGER ABOUT FIXING — IT IS ABOUT STAYING

Earlier in your journey, healing required excavation.

You learned to name patterns, trace wounds, and understand how your nervous system adapted to survive.

That work mattered.

It built the foundation.

But you are no longer living underground.

At this stage, the question is quieter — and more revealing:

How do I stay loyal to myself when nothing is wrong?

This is where many women get confused.

They expect the work to feel intense.

Transformational.

Obvious.

Instead, it feels... neutral.

And neutrality can be unsettling for women who learned to recognize danger as proof they were alive.

Becoming now is not about pushing forward.

It is about not disappearing when life feels calm.

That is the new practice.

THE SHIFT YOU MAY NOT HAVE NOTICED YET

You might not have named it, but your body knows this phase has begun.

You don't feel dramatic pain — you feel subtle misalignment.

You don't panic — you pause.

You don't collapse — you adjust.

You don't spiral — you recalibrate.

You are no longer fighting yourself.

You are learning how to **live with yourself**.

And that requires a different skill than survival ever did.

Survival demanded constant vigilance.

Becoming asks for consistency, presence, and restraint — not from fear, but from respect.

THE PRACTICE IS NOT DISCIPLINE — IT IS RELATIONSHIP

You were already disciplined in survival.

You woke up when you didn't want to.

You endured environments that weren't nourishing.

You adapted constantly.

So this phase is not asking you for more effort.

It is asking for **relationship** —

with your body, your creativity, your time, your energy, and your truth.

The practice of becoming is the daily decision to ask:

What supports the woman I am now?

Not the woman who had to earn safety.

Not the woman who survived by overfunctioning.

Not the woman who proved her worth through endurance.

The woman who exists now.

WHAT BECOMING LOOKS LIKE IN REAL LIFE

Becoming is sustained through small, embodied choices — not grand routines.

It shows up when you notice yourself rushing and choose to slow down.

When irritation rises and you ask what boundary wants to be honored.

When you pause before saying yes and check whether your body agrees.

When you let creativity exist without demanding it "go somewhere."

When you rest without explaining yourself.

When you allow pleasure without justifying it.

None of this is impressive.

That is the point.

This is not the work of performance.

It is the work of **stability**.

LEARNING TO TRUST YOURSELF IN REAL TIME

Self-trust now is not philosophical.

It is practical.

It is built when you honor a preference.

When you follow a quiet instinct.

When you adjust instead of override yourself.

When you choose alignment over explanation.

You do not need to make perfect choices.

You only need to **stay present with the choices you make**, instead of abandoning yourself afterward.

This is how identity solidifies — not through certainty, but through consistency.

CREATIVITY IS NO LONGER ESCAPE — IT IS INTEGRATION

Earlier in your life, creativity may have been refuge.

A place to disappear.

A way to survive.

Now it becomes something else.

Creativity becomes how you **stay connected**.

How you tell the truth gently.

How you integrate your inner and outer life.

This phase may look smaller than you expected.

Five minutes.

A sentence.

A note you don't overthink.

A melody you don't pressure into relevance.

This is not regression.

It is embodiment.

REST IS PART OF THE PRACTICE — NOT A DETOUR FROM IT

At this stage, rest is no longer collapse.

It is maintenance.

You rest because you respect your nervous system.

You rest because you understand what it takes to stay present.

You rest because you are building a life you intend to inhabit.

You are no longer resting to recover from harm.

You are resting to **sustain alignment**.

That is a different relationship entirely.

THE PRACTICE IS NOT LINEAR — AND IT DOESN'T NEED TO BE

Some days you will feel deeply rooted.

Other days you will feel tender.

Some days clarity will arrive easily.

Other days uncertainty will visit again.

None of this means you are going backward.

It means you are living.

Becoming is not about staying elevated.

It is about staying connected —

to yourself, to your truth, to the body you once had to leave.

WHEN YOU FEEL UNSTEADY, RETURN HERE

Not because something is wrong.

But because you are human.

Ask yourself:

Who am I being today?

What does she need right now?

What is one small way I can support her?

That is enough.

Becoming does not require overhaul.

It requires presence.

CLOSING — YOU ARE ALREADY LIVING IT

You do not need to try harder to become yourself.

You only need to stop leaving yourself behind.

Your healing gave you awareness.

Your self-leadership gave you direction.

Your boundaries gave you structure.

Your creativity gave you meaning.

Now this practice — quiet, grounded, ordinary — carries you forward.

You are no longer becoming in theory.
You are becoming in real time.

And in the next chapter, we pause — not to analyze, but to honor.

Because the woman reading these words
is not the woman who started this book.

And she deserves to be acknowledged.

CHAPTER 24 - To The Woman Who Made It Here

A Blessing for Your Becoming
This chapter is for you.

Not the woman you were trying to be.

Not the woman you thought you had to become to survive.

Not the woman who performed for safety, love, or belonging.

This is for the woman reading these words now.

The woman who kept going when no one was watching.

The woman who stayed curious when it would have been easier to shut down.

The woman who chose honesty over numbness.

The woman who did not disappear — even when disappearing felt like relief.

You made it here.

And that matters.

LET YOURSELF BE WITNESSED

Before we move forward, pause.

Let yourself feel this truth without rushing past it:

You did not read this far by accident.

You did not stay because it was easy.

You did not arrive here because your life unfolded gently.

You arrived because something in you refused to abandon yourself.

Even when you were tired.

Even when you doubted your timing.

Even when you wondered if healing was worth the effort.

Even when you questioned whether you were asking for too much.

You stayed.

That tells me something essential about you.

YOU WERE BRAVE IN WAYS NO ONE APPLAUDED

There were no ceremonies for what you endured.

No recognition for the nights you held yourself together.

No audience for the boundaries you learned to set quietly.

No witnesses for the versions of yourself you had to let go of.

But courage does not require an audience to be real.

Your bravery showed up in the moments where you listened instead of numbed.

Where you trusted the discomfort instead of silencing it.

Where you broke patterns you did not create.

Where you allowed grief to move instead of burying it.

Where you stayed soft in a world that trained you toward hardness.

You did not only heal intellectually.

You healed relationally.

You healed somatically.

You healed creatively.

You healed spiritually.

That is not small work.

HEAR THIS CLEARLY

You are not behind.

Not in life.

Not in love.

Not in creativity.

Not in becoming.

You are exactly where a woman arrives when she has done the inner work required to hold herself.

Some people reach milestones early but never learn how to stay.
You took time — and learned how to inhabit your life.

That is not delay.
That is wisdom.

YOU BELONG TO YOURSELF NOW

You no longer have to earn rest.
You no longer have to justify your needs.
You no longer have to explain your boundaries.
You no longer have to shrink to remain acceptable.
You no longer have to disappear to be loved.

You belong to yourself now.
And from that place, everything changes.

A BLESSING FOR WHAT COMES NEXT

May you trust your body when it speaks.
May you listen to your intuition without arguing it into silence.
May you recognize alignment when it arrives — even if it looks unfamiliar.
May you walk away from what no longer fits without rewriting the story to soften it.
May you allow joy without waiting for permission.
May your creativity feel like home, not pressure.
May your voice feel natural, not risky.
May your life feel spacious enough to breathe inside.

And may you remember, on the days you forget, that you did not survive everything you survived to live halfway.

THIS IS NOT THE END — IT IS THE PAUSE

This chapter is not a conclusion.
It is a moment of stillness.
A hand on your back.
A breath before movement resumes.

Ahead of you is integration — not more healing, but coherence.

Ahead of you is authorship — not proving, but choosing.

Ahead of you is a life that no longer orbits your wounds, but your values.

And you are ready for it.

You always were.

FROM ME TO YOU

If no one has ever said *I see you* and meant it — I mean it now.

I see the woman who kept choosing herself.

I see the woman who did not harden.

I see the woman who stayed curious.

I see the woman who made it here.

And I honor her.

Take this moment with you.

The chapters ahead are about living — not healing.

And you are no longer entering them as the woman you used to be.

You are walking forward as the woman you are becoming.

CHAPTER 25 - The Integration Blueprint

How You Keep Living the Woman You Became
Healing changes you.

But integration is what keeps you.

Healing is the breakthrough.

Integration is the living.

It's what you return to on ordinary days — especially the ones where you forget who you are, why you did this work, or how far you've come. It's what steadies you when life gets loud, when old instincts whisper, when familiar patterns try to re-enter through unguarded doors.

This chapter is not about fixing yourself.

It's about staying yourself.

What follows isn't a list of techniques. It's a way of relating to yourself — a simple internal orientation you can return to whenever you feel uncentered, uncertain, or pulled away from your truth.

Think of it as a home base.

THE INTEGRATION BLUEPRINT

Six Anchors for Living From Selfhood

You don't "master" integration.

You return to it.

These anchors aren't rules.

They are places you come back to — gently, repeatedly, without punishment.

1. The Anchor of Presence

Where am I right now?

Integration always begins here.

Not in yesterday.

Not in the story.

Not in what you should already know.

Presence means locating yourself before you try to understand yourself.

It might be as simple as feeling your breath again.

Noticing your body in the chair.

Hearing your own thoughts without immediately reacting to them.

When you feel scattered or overwhelmed, don't analyze first.

Find yourself first.

Presence doesn't fix everything — but it keeps you from leaving yourself while trying.

2. The Anchor of Choice

What would the woman I've become choose here?

This is where identity replaces effort.

You are no longer choosing from fear, conditioning, or inherited survival roles.

You are choosing from self-trust.

Sometimes the choice is quiet.

Sometimes it surprises you.

Would you still say yes to this now?

Would you still stay silent here?

Would you still explain yourself?

You don't need certainty.

You need alignment.

Integration happens every time you choose in support of who you are now — not who you used to be.

3. The Anchor of Boundaries

What protects my energy, time, and truth?

Boundaries are not reactions. They are maintenance. You don't set them because something went wrong. You set them because something matters — you.

Integration looks like leaving before resentment builds.

Saying no without rehearsing a justification.

Choosing rest without guilt.

Disengaging without drama.

Boundaries are how your growth stays real in daily life.

4. The Anchor of Voice

What needs to be expressed instead of swallowed?

Your voice isn't only for speaking.

It's how you stay oriented to yourself.

Expression might look like naming discomfort early.

Writing instead of spiraling.

Creating instead of numbing.

Telling the truth simply, without defending it.

When your voice disappears, your center disappears with it.

Integration requires expression — not performance, not explanation, just honesty.

5. The Anchor of Regulation

What helps my body feel safe right now?

You don't integrate through pressure.

You integrate through safety.

Sometimes that means slowing down.

Sometimes it means moving.

Sometimes it means nourishment, quiet, or rest.

Your body isn't in the way of your becoming.

It's the container for it.

When your body feels safe, your identity stabilizes.

6. The Anchor of Compassion

How do I stay with myself when I stumble?

This is the anchor that makes everything sustainable.

You will forget.

You will regress at times.

You will have days where clarity feels far away.

Compassion says:

I don't abandon myself here.

I don't shame myself for being human.

I return instead of restart.

Integration isn't about never falling back.

It's about coming back faster — and kinder.

HOW TO LIVE THIS BLUEPRINT

You don't use all six anchors at once.

On some days, presence is enough.

On others, boundaries will be the thing that steadies you.

Some days, voice brings you back.

Some days, compassion does.

This isn't a checklist.

It's a relationship — one that keeps you rooted in yourself as life unfolds.

THE TRUTH ABOUT INTEGRATION

Integration isn't dramatic.

It's quiet.

It's steady.

It's ordinary.

And it's powerful.

It's how healing stops being something you *did*
and becomes something you *are*.

You don't need to remember every insight from this book.

You don't need to stay perfectly aligned.

You don't need to get it right.

You only need to know how to return.

And now — you do.

BEFORE WE CLOSE

You are not trying to hold onto a version of yourself.
You are living her.
   And whenever life pulls you outward,
whenever old instincts whisper,
whenever you feel yourself drifting —
   Come back here.
   This is how you keep living the woman you became.

A Final Letter From the Author

A personal send-off
If you're here, still holding this book, I want to begin by saying something simply and clearly:

I see you.

Not the version of you that performs strength.
Not the version of you that survived quietly.
Not the version of you that made things work at great personal cost.

I see the woman who kept going when she didn't yet have language for what was happening inside her. The woman who learned early how to read rooms, manage emotions, and disappear just enough to stay safe — without ever fully leaving herself behind.

The fact that you made it to this page tells me something important about you.

You stayed.
You stayed with discomfort.
You stayed with memory.
You stayed with truth.
You stayed with questions that didn't have quick answers.
You stayed long enough to let something inside you rearrange.

That is not small work.

I didn't write this book because I believe I have all the answers.
I wrote it because I know what it's like to live without mirrors — and what it takes to build them for yourself.

There were many points in my life where I could have hardened.
Where I could have shut down.
Where I could have decided that survival was "good enough."

But something in me — the same thing I recognize in you — kept insisting that there was more life available than the one I had learned how to endure.
Not an easier life.
Not a perfect life.
A truer one.

If this book has done its job, it hasn't given you a new identity.
It's helped you recognize the one you've been protecting all along.

You may not feel healed.
You may not feel finished.
You may still have days where old patterns tug at you and old voices get loud.

That doesn't mean you failed.
It means you're human — and awake.

What matters now is not whether you never fall back into old ways.
What matters is that you know how to return.

Return to your body.
Return to your voice.
Return to your discernment.
Return to the part of you that knows when something is off — and no longer explains it away.

You are not late.
You are not broken.
You are not "too much."

You are a woman who learned how to survive without the support she deserved — and is now learning how to live with intention.

If there's one thing I hope you carry with you after this book, it's this:

You do not need to become someone else to be worthy of peace.
You don't need to perform healing correctly.
You don't need to prove how strong you are.
You don't need to rush your process to make other people comfortable.

You are allowed to move at the pace of integration.
You are allowed to build a life that feels safe and alive.
You are allowed to choose environments, relationships, and rhythms that support who you are now — not who you had to be.

If at any point you forget, come back to what your body knows.
Come back to the truth that you don't disappear anymore.
Come back to the woman who is capable of choosing herself — again and again.

I'm grateful you trusted me with this part of your journey.
I'm honored that you let my words sit beside your lived experience.
And I believe, deeply, in what you're becoming — not because it's impressive, but because it's honest.

This isn't goodbye.
It's simply the moment where I step back and say:

You've got this.
And more importantly — **you've got you.**

With respect, warmth, and solidarity,
Shauntey

About Creatives Unboxed

T here is a moment in every creative's healing where the question quietly shifts from *"What happened to me?"* to *"What can I build from here?"*

When I reached that moment in my own journey, I realized something unexpected: I wasn't simply healing from my past — I was creating the space I needed but never had. A space for people like us. People with big gifts and complicated beginnings. People who learned to create in the dark and bloom without applause.

Creatives Unboxed was born from that realization.

It didn't begin as a business plan. It began as a promise I made to myself — that no creative who carried a mother wound would have to build their dreams alone. I knew what it felt like to work through delayed confidence, to try to make art with a shaken sense of identity, to move through rooms without guidance, to shrink my voice because no one had ever taught me how to trust it.

And I also knew what it felt like when healing finally met purpose — when clarity returned, when confidence rose from discipline, when the creative child inside me stopped whispering and started speaking with her whole chest.

That is the soil from which Creatives Unboxed grew.

Today, it is a sanctuary for creatives who are ready to expand — emotionally, artistically, spiritually, and professionally. Through creative direction, strategy, and guided development,

I help artists and visionary thinkers uncover their voice, strengthen their identity, and build the kind of creative lives that reflect who they truly are — not who trauma trained them to be.

The work is personal.

It is tender.

It is transformative.

But more than anything, it is a continuation of the healing you began in these pages. Because your creativity deserves a home that can hold it — a home built on insight, intention, and emotional safety.

If this book awakened something in you...

If you felt seen, or understood, or suddenly more possible...

If you felt the creative child inside you lift her head for the first time in years...

Creatives Unboxed is where we keep going.

Where the inner work meets the outer calling.

Where your voice becomes vision.

Where your ideas take shape in the real world.

Where your lineage shifts, not just through survival, but through creation.

I built this space for us — for the creatives who were overlooked, undervalued, or under-nurtured... yet still felt a pull to become more. If you're ready for the next chapter of your becoming, you can find me here:

www.creativesunboxed.com

Your healing started in these pages.

Your expansion continues wherever your art takes you next.

And I'm honored to walk a piece of that journey with you.

Shauntey Walker is a writer, creative strategist, and founder of Creatives Unboxed Press. Her work explores the intersection of emotional healing, self-leadership, and creative identity—particularly for women who learned to survive without emotional safety.

Drawing from lived experience and years of personal inquiry, Shauntey writes for women navigating the long aftermath of emotional neglect, helping them move from survival patterns into grounded selfhood. Her work centers on nervous system awareness, boundaries, voice reclamation, and the quiet, practical work of becoming emotionally sovereign.

Rather than offering prescriptive self-help, Shauntey's writing emphasizes integration—how healing is lived, not performed. Her voice is known for its clarity, compassion, and depth, resonating especially with creative women who are ready to stop shrinking and begin leading their lives from truth.

She lives and works in Los Angeles.